Dec 2011

Praise for Marc Miller's best-selling book, *Selling Is Dead*

"You'll find this a thoughtful book. It's provocative and insightful. *Selling Is Dead* presents a new and useful perspective on creating and managing large selling opportunities. And like most books that make you think, it's not a quick read. But its ideas are worthwhile and will repay the effort."
—**Neil Rackham, consultant and business thinker, author of *SPIN Selling***

"A collaborative and commercial approach that is a key element of the growth journey. *Selling Is Dead* not only addresses the importance of a team-focused selling framework, but other critical success factors as well."
—**Damian A. Thomas, general manager and corporate sales leader, General Electric Company**

"*Selling Is Dead* is a wonderful blend of balanced, forward thinking, and practical common-sense guidance on how to mutually win with your customer in today's highly competitive marketplace. Planning from your buyer's point of view to make them more productive and competitive is critical in large account sales . . . and this book will show you how."
—**David N. Townshend, senior vice president of global sales, Marriott International**

"The authors articulate the dichotomy of the large sales challenge. Like most companies, our business units at Siemens have unique selling challenges. This is an insightful book that teaches salespeople how to identify, adapt, and adjust to the type of large sales in which they are engaged."
—**Thomas Poole, regional vice president, Siemens Medical Solutions**

A SEAT *at the* TABLE

How Top Salespeople Connect *and*
Drive Decisions *at the* Executive Level

MARC MILLER

GREENLEAF
BOOK GROUP PRESS

Published by Greenleaf Book Group Press
Austin, Texas
www.greenleafbookgroup.com

Distributed by Greenleaf Book Group LLC

For ordering information or special discounts for bulk purchases, please contact Greenleaf Book Group LLC at PO Box 91869, Austin, TX 78709, (512) 891-6100.

Design and composition by Greenleaf Book Group LLC
Cover design by Greenleaf Book Group LLC

Publisher's Cataloging-in-Publication Data
(Prepared by The Donohue Group, Inc.)

Miller, Marc (Marc T.)
    A seat at the table : how top salespeople connect and drive decisions at the executive level / Marc Miller. — 1st ed.

    p. ; cm.
    ISBN: 978-1-929774-69-2

1. Selling. 2. Sales personnel. 3. Success in business. I. Title.
HF5438.25 .M56555 2009
658.85   200894385

Part of the Tree Neutral™ program, which offsets the number of trees consumed in the production and printing of this book by taking proactive steps, such as planting trees in direct proportion to the number of trees used: www.treeneutral.com

TreeNeutral

Printed in the United States of America on acid-free paper

09 10 11 12   10 9 8 7 6 5 4 3 2 1

First Edition

CONTENTS

ACKNOWLEDGMENTS

To my family and parents: Jack, Ann, and my children Jenny, Jason, James, Marc, Jeannete, and Julia. I am blessed with great parents and wonderful children.

To the great folks at O.C. Tanner: Kent Murdock and all his talented associates. But especially John McVeigh, a great leader and risk taker.

To Dolf Kahle, David Peckinpaugh, Tom Hobson, Chris Peer, Gabriel Torok, and Bill Hinsch. But especially Mark Woodka for his continued help and strategic guidance.

To my partners Dave Kelly and Joe Palmisano—thank you.

To Greenleaf Book Group: Clint, Tanya, Alan, Ryan, Kristen. But especially Lari Bishop, editor extraordinaire. This book, in its current form, would not have been possible without her.

A special thanks to my partners at Livescribe: Tim, Eric, Joyce, Byron, and Jim Marggraff. But especially Frank Moura, my new partner, for his help and faith in this new application.

To my associates Jeff and Donna. But especially to Lisa Banach, for never complaining when asked to go above and beyond. Thank you.

And last to my wife Janet for all her support. Without her understanding, patience, and love, writing this book would not have been possible.

CHAPTER ONE
GAME CHANGE

Connecting to customer strategy is a game changer. This is not selling as usual. In fact, it's the opposite. When done properly, the client no longer sees you as a salesperson. You are now a businessperson focused exclusively on helping the customer achieve their strategic goals. And when that shift occurs, everything—and I mean everything—changes.

—John McVeigh, senior vice president of global sales, O.C. Tanner Corporation

LET'S BE FRANK—SELLING HAS an ugly connotation, even *consultative* selling. New research indicates that senior executives do not see salespeople as consultative at all—at least not consultants who can drive or grow their businesses. Instead, they see a group with blinders on—myopically focused on making the short-term sale that adds little value to the mission of their customer's enterprise. Candidly, how do you feel about those stockbrokers cold-calling you in the middle of the day? Do you really believe those people are worthy of your time, or have your best interest at heart? Unfortunately—justifiably or not—these are the people you are compared to when reaching out to new executives and prospects that you could help, given the chance.

This voice-of-customer research delivers both good and bad news for salespeople. The bad news is that business executives and corporate customers feel that far too many salespeople are tactical product-pushers disengaged from the real meaning and purpose of their organizations. These salespeople may have a genuine desire to help, but the help is in the wrong areas. This makes them a well-intentioned group, but misaligned and disconnected from what the customer really cares about.

Now here's the good news. All of the difficulties companies are facing in our turbulent, constantly shifting economy are actually creating the opportunity of a lifetime for salespeople—specifically, the opportunity to play a far more important role in the lives of the customers on whom they call. For those special salespeople who embrace this new role, the world will be one of endless opportunity. Their customers will see them as *difference makers*, champions who deliver value far surpassing that of any single product or service.

And there is even better news. There is new evidence to suggest that salespeople can transcend their current "brand" as product peddlers to achieve record levels of productivity. But, to do this, they must accept one simple truth:

The only thing your customer cares about is value.

The last page of this book states this in large print. Copy it and give it to everyone who talks to customers. It is the most important principle you'll read in these pages.

Based on this truism, there is only one foolproof strategy to drastically improve sales productivity. To achieve radically better sales results, you must become radically more valuable to customers—*strategically* valuable. This growth strategy trumps all others. The game has changed, and new research suggests customers are pleading for a new and different type of value from salespeople and account managers. And, when this new value is created, captured, and delivered, customers no longer view salespeople as salespeople at all. They now see "businesspeople who sell"—those worthy of a seat at their table.

EARNING A SEAT AT THE TABLE

Customers today are looking for value in the form of help—specifically, strategic help. Corporations are under duress as never before—business failure and executive turnover are at an all time high, and business models need adjusting not once every year, but seemingly every week. And executives—people not unlike you and me—often get lost in this rapid pace of change. They need to focus on the future, but the day to day of running a business is like gravity, a force that continuously drags them down into the daily muck, battling the fires necessary to drive short-term results. As a result, senior executives often get off track, becoming disconnected from the real purpose of their organizations—to sustain profitable growth.

And this is where you come in. You have an opportunity to play a new role, and that new role has two distinct parts. First, you have to help executives reconnect to their strategies. When you help customers reconnect to what's important, you connect to them. It's that simple. Second, you need to devise solutions that will help them achieve or expand their master strategic plan. When you suggest solutions that add value to critical customer strategies, you leave competitors in the dust. Since your competition is myopically focused on selling products and services that add little value to the bigger picture strategy of the customer, these traditional competitors will no longer even be on your radar of competition.

To help you prepare yourself for this new role, I'm going to teach you how to quit talking about expenses (products and services) and start having discussions about investments (productivity and differentiation). From the perspective of the executives you will be calling, these are polar opposites. I'm also going to show you how easy it is to comprehend your customer's strategies and connect your products and services to them. And this is how you will earn a seat at the table—that lofty position that executives reserve for those special businesspeople who add strategic value, who make a profound impact on their results, their enterprises, and their people.

When you have a seat, you are seen as an investment, not an expense. You become the type of person customer executives seek for advice before making the big-bet decisions that forever shape the future of their enterprises. When you sit at the table of strategy, you are always welcome.

Most important, when you gain a seat at the table, sales productivity will rise *significantly* because of your ability to do the following:

1. **Protect the core:** Customer executives who consider you to be strategically valuable will not let their internal procurement people reduce the relationship to the lowest common denominator—that is, a cheaper price! Ensuring that senior executives view your solutions as mission critical to their strategies will fortify your relationship with them. That will protect the consistent sales of your core products that you and your company rely on—and that are facing tougher competition in our globalized, transparent, and commoditized economy.

2. **Gain access:** When you have earned a seat at the table, you will be able to connect with more senior executives—the ones who can make big-bet, discretionary, risk/reward decisions that affect your offerings. Executives will not refer salespeople to their colleagues inside or outside of their companies, but they will gladly introduce "strategic advisors" to other executives. It's that simple.

3. **Create demand:** Creating demand for new products and solutions is the platinum competence of the very best sellers. This often requires building a case for change with multiple executives and decision makers. When you show executives that you not only understand their strategy but also can add significant value to it, you're halfway to constructing a rock-solid foundation for change. And this will help protect you from the ubiquitous "no decision" loss of a sale that we all face in long sales cycles.

4. **Get the best of both worlds:** When you successfully add value to the strategies of executives, you are able both to protect your core and to sell the new, without having to sacrifice one opportunity for the other. In other words, commodity products are protected and new solutions are sold. This happens in lockstep, because you are creating a valuable relationship with the client, and the client doesn't want to lose you.

How will you accomplish these things? That's what I intend to teach you—in specific detail, not broad generalities and philosophical bromides. Everyone knows they should be calling on more senior executives, but few know exactly how to do it. That is the mission of this book.

THE ALCHEMY OF CONNECTION

As a salesperson, you are in a constant battle for scarce budgetary dollars. And the best way to access a larger share of those dollars is to connect with senior executives—those within an organization who have the ability to make discretionary spend decisions outside of standard budgets. Since strategy—and the execution of strategy—is what executives weight most important, this is your fastest way to make a quick connection. To help you do this, I'll give you two critical tools:

1. **A simple model:** I will first give you a very simple model that will enable you to quickly cut through the clutter of strategy, focusing on the big picture first. When you can *visually* condense the strategy of a large, complex company onto a single sheet of paper, you will have a newfound power to connect the value you offer to all the stakeholders in a large decision and their big picture strategies.

2. **A simple process:** I will then give you the tools you need to nail the first few calls with executives. It is important to understand that sales success or failure is ultimately determined by what happens early in the selling cycle—not later. You can't gain closure if you can't open. Research has clearly shown that it's what happens *early on* that ultimately makes or breaks your ability to gain traction with senior executives.

Regarding this last point, investing time early on in a relationship to learn strategies, objectives, and challenges has another important benefit: it radically shortens potentially long selling cycles. Being patient on purpose early reduces the risk of opportunities spinning on endlessly at the back end of the cycle—the place where vast sales resources are wasted, according to current sales research. This counterintuitive solution to the classic long-cycle problem requires you to document the strategy of the client early on, and then clearly connect your solutions to their strategic direction.

What I'm going to teach you—and I've done this for thousands of salespeople—is how to uncover a company's strategy quickly. Once you learn the strategy of an organization, you've cracked the code. Immediately, you'll recognize multiple ways to add value to the customer, from bringing new resources to the table, to suggesting some simple services that would be helpful, to suggesting a more intricate and thorough total solution. In other words—and this is important—you don't have to have *all* of the answers. You just have to know what questions to ask that will help you both understand the master plan of the customer and unearth why the organization spends its resources as it does (hint: strategy dictates spend).

EXERCISE

When you've lost large opportunities in the past, whom did you lose to? Did you lose to traditional competition, or the real enemy of many sellers—"no decision"? For sellers who must create demand for new applications—*new ways of doing things*—the real enemy is often buyer inaction or lack of inertia. These can be disappointing losses—and difficult to resurrect once momentum is lost.

CASE STUDIES

Case studies are an important dimension of this book. They reflect the variety of companies that have been deeply engaged in the effort to transition their sales teams. This shift has required salespeople to move from selling tangible products to selling intangible strategic concepts, from selling $1,500 industry-norm products to selling $100,000 vanguard solutions, and from selling to mid-level managers to consulting with senior executives. Many experts in the sales industry would say that such a transformation is almost impossible, yet many companies have done it—companies like O.C. Tanner, MasterCard, Trimble, Fairfield, and more. These companies have proved the experts wrong. They have transformed their salespeople into "businesspeople who sell," and the bottom-line results have exceeded even the most optimistic of expectations.

For your learning purposes, I will refer to these best-practices sales teams—like the following discussion of O.C. Tanner—as a means to reinforce some key strategies, skills, and steps you'll need to learn to successfully connect with your customers strategically at senior executive levels.

A Best-Practices Sales Team

O.C. Tanner (OCT) is a market leader in the recognition rewards industry with about $350 million in revenues. The core offering of the company is long-term service awards, a product category sold to mid-level managers in the human resources and benefits departments. Due to increased competition, growth had flattened over the last decade, and profit margins were slowly deteriorating. Procurement departments were also a stronger voice in decisions, putting even more pressure on price integrity. As a result, the company leadership, guided by CEO Kent Murdoch, created a bold new differentiation strategy based on total recognition solutions.

John McVeigh, senior vice president of global sales, OCT, was ultimately tasked with the transformation of the sales team. He knew that a successful transition would require his approximately 150 salespeople to learn to create demand for the new total recognition solutions. This was a new sandbox—it would require teaching senior leaders in client companies how to use soft and ambiguous appreciation as a strategic mechanism that could help them achieve mission-critical objectives. But this would require selling to human resource executives at least two or three levels up from the mid-level relationships OCT already had in place. And this new total solution approach would go far beyond simple products; training, services, and technology would be important pieces of each configured customer solution. The stakes were large: often the opportunities they were shooting for would be ten times the size of an average service award sale.

Although not without its challenges, this sales force transition was remarkably successful. The core business was maintained as the new differentiation strategy was successfully implemented and the total solutions were sold. Today, the company is now on a fast revenue growth track, and employees are infused with a new sense of energy and excitement. In 2008, the company achieved record growth, and 2009 looks to be an even more impressive year in a very turbulent economy. Customers like Pepsi, Avis, and Quest Diagnostics are seeing important results by leveraging O.C. Tanner solutions to drive employee productivity. Consequently, even in an incredibly disruptive and difficult economy, customers of O.C. Tanner are reluctant to displace a relationship so connected to their mission critical strategies.

ARE YOU READY?

This is a book for salespeople who are ready to go beyond "normal" selling to succeed. That said, it has something to offer all salespeople, particularly those who

- Sell complex offerings—total solutions that have big tickets and long sales cycles
- Sell divergent offerings—products and services that present radically new ways for customers to accomplish their work, and thus require building a case for change at the highest levels
- Sell mature, core offerings—commodities that require consistently new and innovative sales techniques to avoid being reduced to negotiations based solely on price

This is a book about how you can add high-impact value to your customers. This makes it relevant for all salespeople since value is all the customer cares about. Adding high-impact value is possible for all salespeople—even those selling intensely competitive commodity products. But adding high-impact value will require salespeople to do things differently, winning as much or more by *business expertise* as by the products and services being sold. Salespeople may not control products, but they do control their own know-how. That said, if understanding how to better connect and add value to customer strategy as a means to radically improve your sales sounds intriguing to you, then you're going to find this book incredibly valuable.

In a nutshell, that is what this book is all about—understanding how to help your customers win, win bigger, and win more often. When this happens, you win, win bigger, and win more often. You will achieve radical sales productivity improvement and a differentiated position because you added value to the productivity and differentiation strategies of your customers. They win—you win. End of story.

Are you ready to take *your* seat at the table?

CHAPTER TWO

A NEW ROLE, A NEW MIND-SET

For us, it's all about helping the client achieve their objectives first. That's the order—client first, us second. If they win, we win. It's that simple. This is exactly the mind-set of our very best salespeople. I also believe this mind-set—and sales process—truly differentiates our company.

—Paul Schleuter, executive vice president, global sales, Oerlikon/Fairfield

ALL SALESPEOPLE BELIEVE THEY ARE strategically valuable to clients. This is because *strategic value*—much like the discipline of *strategy* itself—is poorly defined. Salespeople mistake strategic value for product value. Comparing the two is akin to comparing apples and oranges.

Product value is about "cheaper-better-faster." In other words, once a product or service category is budgeted, customers always turn their attention to "price-quality-service" attributes. Product value is specifically relevant to mid-level personnel and procurement people tasked with maintaining the day-to-day operations of a company. Senior executives have little interest in product value, understanding that only incremental gain can be achieved by switching vendors. Accordingly, they delegate these tactical decisions to lower-ranking associates.

Strategic value is about something entirely different: differentiation and productivity. Offering strategic value in the form of improved differentiation and increased productivity is the new role salespeople must play. I'm going to give you a process for understanding and embracing this new role, but the very first step you must take is changing your perception of and attitude about what it means to be a salesperson.

UNLEARNING TO SELL, LEARNING TO HELP

The purpose of a salesperson has always been to create and keep a customer. This will never change. What is being challenged now is how accomplishing these two important functions is best done. This has little to do with understanding how to *sell* and everything to do with understanding how customers *buy*.

Buyers are no longer dependent on salespeople to make effective buying decisions. For example, the Internet enables vendor sourcing, search engines allow product comparisons, and reverse auctions drive the cheapest buy. All these procurement mechanisms are fairly recent phenomena. As a result, buyers are now beginning to ask, "Do we really need to see salespeople anymore?" If you believe they aren't asking this question, just read the Wal-Mart case study in the next chapter.

These disrupters have radically changed the traditional job of salespeople. In the past, the job was calling on mid-level functional departments to sell someone something. Not anymore. The new sales job requires more time spent calling on senior-level executives—not to sell a product, but to help the customer get better results.

Unfortunately, calling on executives is a whole new game for many salespeople. To successfully engage at senior levels, salespeople need to abandon the old ways—in effect, *unlearn* to sell. This means letting go of the "sell something to someone" mind-set so pervasive among product myopic sellers who cannot see the bigger picture of customer value beyond their products. Instead, the salesperson focus must shift—uncompromisingly—to connecting and adding value to client strategy. We'll begin the discussion of how to do this in the next chapter.

For many salespeople, this new mind-set is not only counterintuitive, it is also incomprehensible. You can hear the incredulity now: "Whoa, my job is to sell, right? You're asking me . . . *not* to sell?"

Exactly! For sales revenues to lift, selling must end and helping must begin. No doubt, helping a client achieve radically better results often requires a different sales mind-set. You will need to

- Focus less on how you influence clients and more on how you impact their businesses
- Shift from competing with other vendors to creating value for your client
- Concentrate less on making a sale and more on making a difference

In other words, the mind-set must be on helping the client. This means listening, understanding, and, on occasion, telling the customer that change might not be in their best interest. It means delivering a new kind of help that is more about expertise and know-how than products and services, a kind of help that touches every facet of a business:

- Knowledge *help*
- Brainstorming *help*

- Idea *help*
- Analytic *help*
- Creativity *help*
- Collaborative *help*
- Strategic *help*

For some, this attitude is tantamount to sales heresy. In reality, the authenticity that comes from a genuine desire to help the client shows through.

BEYOND CERTAINTY

In his wonderful book *Beyond Certainty: The Changing Worlds of Organizations* (Harvard Business School Press, 1996), Charles Handy perfectly described the creative mind-set necessary to engage a client in discussions about enabling their differentiation strategy:

> When I went to school, I did not learn anything much except for the hidden message that every major problem in life had already been solved . . . For years afterward, when confronted with a problem that was new to me, I ran for an expert. It never occurred to me . . . that I might come up with my own answers . . . The world is not an unsolved puzzle waiting for the occasional genius to unlock its secrets. The world, or most of it, is an empty space waiting to be filled. That realization changed my life . . . I was free to try out my own ideas, invent my own scenarios, and create my own futures.

This self-actualizing prose speaks to the belief that a salesperson trying to become a client advisor must embrace—that there are no predetermined answers. There is no *certainty*—no expert with the definitive solution.

This attitude requires a leap of faith for many salespeople. For instance, many salespeople are skeptical of their abilities to influence a senior executive to consider a new way of doing things. They believe a customer executive will not make a high-risk decision without proof, without the *certainty of supporting data*. This self-limiting belief actually prevents salespeople from doing their new jobs, of engaging different executives in different discussions about different ways of doing things.

In reality, this lack-of-data argument lacks veracity. Logically, if data were available to unequivocally prove a value proposition, no differentiated position could be achieved by the customer. Competition would have already adopted the solution (that would be the source of the data), negating any first-mover advantage.

We see it time and again with those who practice a better way of market facing. Companies and clients like O.C. Tanner, Trimble, Nokia, Procter & Gamble (P&G), and Fairfield "get" that the X factor in creating customer value—solutions that genuinely help the client achieve something distinctive and remarkable—begins in the open and possibility-driven mind-set of the connector—the salesperson.

That said, an open, helping mind-set will not compensate for lack of an effective strategy. Until you extinguish blissful ignorance, outcomes will remain static. Attitude changes when one learns the proper way and compares it to current reality—ego removed.

For example, my daughter plays the cello. Her belief was that she played the cello well. Upon hearing a brilliant soloist play, she commented, "So that's what a cello sounds like." A lightbulb went on. She had grasped the contrast between mediocrity and mastery, the first step on her performance-improvement journey. Now she needs to take some risks by trying some different techniques, getting feedback, and adjusting. She's on her way.

Whoever said "life belongs to the discontent" half nailed it. In other words, to play at the highest level—the senior executive level—you will need not only the right mind-set but also the proper methodology to follow. One without the other just won't cut it. And, just like my cello-playing daughter, you're going to have to take some risks, get some feedback, and adjust before your attitude will make the total shift.

DO THEY WANT OUR HELP?

Are executives open to salespeople helping them improve their strategies or their strategic success rates? Absolutely. And numerous interviews and surveys prove it.

Dave Kelly is CEO of Physicians Imaging Solutions. Kelly's company partners with large physician groups and hospitals to help them offer diagnostic imaging services to their customers. That means that all the big MRI companies—GE, Siemens, Phillips, Hitachi, Toshiba—call on his company to sell their MRI equipment. Kelly wants to work with salespeople who are willing to look at a bigger strategic picture. Unfortunately, says Kelly, the big MRI manufacturers don't seem to employ such salespeople—with one exception.

> The best—and only—salesperson who ever called on us who could have a strategic dialogue was Martin Steinman of Siemens. Martin was unique. I remember the first time he called on us. He said, "I don't know much about you, but I'd like to understand your business, go out on calls

if necessary, and learn not only what differentiates you, but why customers buy from you. Ultimately, I'd like to learn what's important to you, and whether we might fit into that picture."

We do many, many projects with large physician groups and hospitals that require thoughtful, custom solutions. After learning about a specific project in depth, Martin would come back with ideas that would enhance that vision. Every other salesperson talked about MRI hardware. Martin got into all the elements around the MRI that I knew would make or break a successful project: service aspects, installation, logistics, marketing, financial, and physical location. If we had eight objectives to achieve within a project, we might do five and Martin would take responsibility for the other three. His solutions were always creative and thoughtful. Most important, his ideas and solutions always reflected what we were strategically trying to accomplish as a company.

Every time Martin came in, he worked hard at listening and learning. It was never transactional. All the other salespeople who called on us would ask the same thing: "Do you have any deals happening?" Frankly, in comparison to Martin, they were simpletons, always focused on the tactical. They never engaged us in business conversations. That's why we did all of our business with Martin.

The difference between Martin Steinman and other salespeople was pretty significant. To me, Martin was in business development, not sales. His focus was clearly on developing my business, not selling a piece of million-dollar hardware. I can honestly say that Martin enabled us to grow our revenues by freeing us up to do more deals.

The reality is that if the companies who sell to us don't send us the right salespeople to work with, we all end up underoptimized. Call it lose-lose. In reality, MRI and diagnostic hardware, although costing millions, is really just a commodity, and if the salespeople we deal with can't see beyond this, we end up negotiating pricing and terms accordingly. We pay for value, period. And, it's so much better to work with a salesperson and company who add value beyond products by synergistically aligning with our strategies.

As mentioned earlier, all salespeople believe they are strategically valuable to customers. They believe they are already helping. Unfortunately, the evidence proves otherwise, as shown by a landmark survey conducted by MasterCard. And possibly the more compelling revelation was that executives have a genuine desire for salespeople to help them improve their strategies or strategic success rates.

A New Enemy

The B2B division of MasterCard operates in the extremely competitive credit card business—an industry full of cost-cutting rivalry and me-too products. Looking for ways to differentiate itself in a crowded sphere, MasterCard asked more than one thousand of its key business customers an important question: What value would they like to receive more of from their MasterCard salesperson? The results were eye-popping. In a resounding vote of need, customers requested MasterCard salespeople help in more strategic ways:

- Competitive strategy: learn my industry sphere to help me gain competitive advantage

- Strategic thinking: less problem solving, more thought leadership
- Innovation: customize solutions that enable us to take advantage of new opportunities and enter different markets
- Alignment: develop new program strategies that tie more closely to our growth and profitability objectives

When the final numbers were tabulated, corporate customers rated MasterCard salespeople a paltry 4.1 on a scale of 1 to 10 on their ability to deliver strategic value. In other words, what customers felt was lacking was the ability of MasterCard salespeople to drive the customers' businesses. Service was fine, as was problem solving, but these were simply tactical expectations of the customer, not value adds. It was a rude awakening for MasterCard leadership, who were hoping for something closer to a 10.

But the real lesson for MasterCard executives—and sellers—came later. Before releasing the results of their findings, MasterCard executives decided to take one more step. They asked MasterCard salespeople to rate themselves in the very same category in which customers felt they received frustratingly little value—*delivery of strategic advice.*

How do you think the three hundred–plus MasterCard salespeople rated themselves on their abilities to create and capture strategic value to key corporate customers? Take a guess—5.0? 6.0? 7.0? 8.0? 8.5? 9.0? Guess again. The salespeople gave their strategic value–creation abilities a 9.9!

Upon seeing the results, MasterCard leadership realized they had just encountered a new enemy—the distorted belief system of their sales and account management teams. This foe would be far more formidable than any traditional competitor in the company's attempt to become more strategically valuable to customers. To quote the famous words of Pogo cartoonist Walt Kelly, MasterCard "had met the enemy, and [they realized] he is us."

FLAWED SELF-ASSESSMENT

Social psychologists call the phenomenon of misjudging one's own competence, importance, and value to others as "flawed self-assessment." In other words, individuals generally consider themselves smarter, more powerful, and more indispensable than they really are. From this perspective, most people have a good reputation—*with themselves!*

Companies often fail to optimize customer wallets due to the flawed self-assessment of their field sales force. As a result, they fail to reach their true potential. For instance, contrast two different salespeople in two different territories. Salesperson A generates $2 million in revenue from a single customer who buys the entire mix of products and services sold by the company—a bundled total solution. The total potential of this customer is $2 million, so customer potential is wholly optimized.

Salesperson B—a proud veteran who often tells others that he is a self-made man—sells three times as much, $6 million, to a different customer in a different territory. This is one of the largest accounts in the company, vaulting Salesperson B into the top ranks of sellers year after year. By most accounts, this salesperson is doing an excellent job—triple the results of Salesperson A. His "top ten" rank qualifies him for the "big trip" every year—a recognition that affirms his peer status as one of the best salespeople in the company.

Yet, upon closer examination, a different story emerges. The $6 million customer of Salesperson B buys only products—no services. And, in this particular account, profit margins have been steadily shrinking as procurement has wrapped their price-squeezing arms around the product category, products being easy prey when no services are involved. In addition, if one considers the total solution approach with this customer, this customer has the potential to generate $30 million in revenue, meaning that $24 million has been unrealized because of Salesperson B's product-based approach. "I am doing all I can," Salesperson B proudly protests to his line manager, "and I think I should be commended for holding onto the core business in such a competitive market." Behind the scenes, he also protests to the other veterans that "the new changes are a waste of time. Just wait, we'll revert back to the old product ways in no time at all." Sales leadership, of course, view the reality of Salesperson B in reverse—marginally profitable business with only 20 percent of total customer potential being realized.

The point of the story is not that Salesperson A is the real hero who should be recognized (she is and should be). The real lesson is that Salesperson B—the acknowledged self-made man apparently in awe of his own maker—will never make the transition to selling total solutions until self-assessment changes and the blinders of "product value" are removed. And until then, customer potential will remain just potential.

This type of flawed self-assessment manifests itself in an interesting way in the sales forecasting process. In most sales forces, the bottom quartile of salespeople are those most guilty of unwarranted optimism—they vastly overinflate the probability of success. In other words, less competent salespeople are extremely poor forecasters because they do not recognize their own deficiencies. In this regard, they are doubly handicapped.

Surprisingly, the top quartile of salespeople actually forecast in reverse—they demonstrate a tendency to be more pessimistic about opportunities. In effect, they lowball their chances of success. This leads to more accurate forecasts—primarily due to the fact that higher performers have a tendency to have a more accurate sense of self. In this manner, they are doubly advantaged.

This is the reality of flawed self-assessment: Until salespeople understand that they can be an actual barrier to delivering new, more strategic value to customers, the organizations that employ them will never realize their true potential. This ties flawed self-assessment to the most critical challenge facing every twenty-first-century organization—sustaining profitable growth. Put another way, salespeople who do not understand how to add strategic value negatively impact both the sustainability efforts of their organizations *and* the customers on whom they call. Flawed self-assessment, in this case, can be a very sharp, double-edged sword.

EXERCISE

What would your customers say if asked whether you truly under-stand—and connect to—their mission-critical strategies? Would they say that you understand their competitive sphere, their unique positioning, and how they intend to separate themselves from the competition? Finally, how would your customers rate you on your ability to deliver strategic value on a scale of 1 (low) to 10 (high)? When evaluating yourself, don't make the same mis-takes other overoptimistic salespeople do. Don't let flawed self-assessment get in the way of reality. Look through your records for proof of your score.

Mirror, Mirror, on the Wall . . .

How do you get a better handle on your true competency level? Let me give you an example.

Every three years or so, I send out an e-mail to a dozen con-fidants and customers, usually a rotating list, asking them to describe my true uniqueness, plus things I should "avoid" doing (weaknesses). I am always amazed by how much I learn about myself from this simple exercise. People who know you best typically have a much better sense of your strengths and weaknesses than you do. In other words, living in your own skin means that sometimes you can't see the forest for the trees.

What have I learned about myself? One thing I have learned is that I'm really not a very good manager. I do not enjoy spending my time managing the day-to-day of a business, doing the important supervisory tasks that drive employee performance. It's just not how I'm wired, being much more comfortable in the world of ideas than that of daily productivity of associates.

When I first heard this feedback, it was a bit ego bruising. Not a good manager? Me? But in the end, the news was liberating. Today, my associates and partners do the managing. This allows me to spend my time in other areas—speaking to groups of salespeople and sales leaders, writing books, and consulting with senior sales executives faced with transitioning their sales teams—all activities I enjoy immeasurably.

I would strongly encourage you to do this valuable exercise—it can lead to some profound changes in your career. In other words, do a 360-degree assessment of yourself. It will take you about five minutes to write an e-mail and send it out to ten or twenty people. Make sure to include your sales manager and/ or higher-level executives in your company who know you well. You might also want to include a handful of customers. In effect, you're conducting the MasterCard research—on yourself!

The key point here is that you want to spend your time doing those things you naturally do best. And, although no one wants to spend time in areas where they do not have natural aptitudes, the reality of selling may require you to shore up key weaknesses in critical job areas. A feedback mechanism can help you realize what you do best, what you should be doing more of, and what you don't do so well and should either improve—or delegate away. Feedback from others keeps you firmly grounded in both of these realities.

A HIGHER STANDARD

Salespeople are usually okay with change—as long as it's the other guy. Our salespeople now know that this attitude will not work at O.C. Tanner. We're in a constant state of change in our quest to be the value leader in our markets. It's a commitment that starts at the very top. Leaders have to demonstrate that we're willing to roll up our sleeves and delve into those small details that ultimately separate the best from the rest.

—John McVeigh, senior vice president of global sales, O.C. Tanner

Self-evaluation mechanisms like the one described above take courage. But when you see the results, they are thought provoking, fun, and rewarding. This is comparable to having a personal board of directors—all working on making you better. Ultimately, the feedback you receive forces you to hold yourself up to a higher standard. In selling, that can be difficult to do. Selling is still considered a "social science," and many still believe sales cannot be taught (although there is evidence stating otherwise).

I would suggest using the competency framework described in this book as a mirror—one that forces honest reflectivity. When you compare yourself to a proven discipline or methodology, you become your own harshest critic. I do not hold myself up as a maestro, but the selling effectiveness framework you'll read in these pages has a proven research base and strong track record of success. That makes it a worthy measuring stick if your goal is to add strategic value to customers.

CHAPTER THREE
VELCRO VALUE

Everyone wants to remove problems, but this isn't what really gets traction at the senior executive level. It's attaching to—and enabling—the client vision that really grabs attention. This is the world of new possibilities, huge opportunities, and unlimited potential.

—Peter Ryan, executive vice president of global sales and services,
Sun Microsystems

I LOVE VELCRO. IN FACT, I'M A VELCRO GUY. Look up *Velcro* in any dictionary and you'll see my picture—I'm the poster boy for this fascinating material. This affinity can drive my wife a bit crazy as I often use the quick fix solutions of Velcro to get a job done.

Wikipedia describes Velcro as hook-and-loop fastener. If you look closely at this unique material, you'll see two dissimilar surfaces. One surface has thousands of tiny hooks. The other surface has thousands of tiny loops. When you press the two together, an instant bond occurs. It's like magic.

In similar fashion, you will need to "make like Velcro" to ensure that your complex solutions stick with your customers. Think of the fuzzy Velcro surface that has hundreds of loops as representing all of the client strategies—a few big ones along with dozens to hundreds of substrategies. The loops represent these many client initiatives and strategies.

The other Velcro surface—the coarse one with the hooks—is your value proposition. A single value proposition adds many, many different types of customer value. It removes a variety of problems, helps different departments in very different ways, and enables the accomplishment of multiple strategies. Now, think of each single Velcro hook as representing these many individual value elements.

Your job is to simply bring the two together, making sure the proper "value connections" are made with those people who have an important voice in the decision. When this happens—instant connection!

I'm getting ahead of myself a bit, but here's an important rule of thumb in the process of selling large, high-risk offerings. Ready? The more client strategies you can put your value hooks into, the better. Put another way, the odds of your value proposition gaining acceptance is directly correlated to your ability to connect unique strains of value to the many stakeholders in a decision. It's pretty logical stuff—the more value connections, the better.

But before you can "make like Velcro," you're going to have to learn how to align your side with the client's side: how to make the connection in a way that will stick. To do this you need to learn a little bit more about what generates the Velcro surface with all the loops—the fuzzy client strategies.

NEW CUSTOMER REALITIES

The real takeaway of the MasterCard research presented in chapter 2 is that today's customer not only needs but also is *actively requesting* a different kind of help. Customers and prospects are looking for the salespeople who call on them to connect and add value to their strategies.

Discovering the drivers of this common need is the first step salespeople must take in becoming strategically valuable and connecting with executives.

Senior executives are under enormous pressure today. Executive compensation is way up—and the board and stockholders have little tolerance for poor C-suite performance. Customers, especially senior executives, are under enormous pressure today to deliver on two fronts:

1. **The Province of Productivity,** where senior executives must deliver the quarterly and annual numbers that satisfy all of the stakeholders—not an easy task. Productivity is about generating more with less, such as expense-reduction programs, improved process efficiencies, and lean quality initiatives. The end game for productivity is a competitively advantageous cost structure.

2. **The Domain of Differentiation,** where senior executives must ensure that the enterprise is well positioned for the future—an even more daunting challenge. Differentiation means creating new offerings, entering different markets, or devising any new strategy that leads to competitive separation, higher growth, and the ultimate reward, premium profit margins.

Productivity and differentiation are the two major executive decision categories that drive scores of subdecisions within an enterprise. Think of differentiation as the "growth numerator" and productivity as the "cost denominator." What links the two—and grabs the attention of senior executives—is that both have significant impact on the ability of the organization to sustain profitable growth. This is why senior executives spend a great deal of time thinking about these two critical areas of their businesses.

Although these two elements must work in harmony if the company is to be successful, each has a very large appetite for corporate resources. The job of the executive is to make sure that each is appropriately fed and to avoid overfeeding one at the expense of the other.

At the same time, executives must balance the urgent (today) with the important (tomorrow). Although this has never been an easy task, it's a new set of disrupters that are making things perilous for today's executives. Call these disruptive elements the "new realities." All the realities I'm about to describe have monumental impact on all organizations. No individual or company will escape the pull of these forces. Consequently, they cause all senior executives to rethink their master plans for sustaining profitable growth. As you read this list, I hope you reach a critical breakthrough—every one of these realities affects your company as much as it does your customers. Every problem your customer faces, you face.

- **Transparency:** immediate Internet sourcing that generates names of hundreds of cheaper-priced competitors
- **Standardization:** new RFP and reverse-auction (RA) processes that pit vendors against each other in price duels
- **Reverse engineering:** new technologies that enable competitors to copycat products in months, weeks, days . . . minutes
- **Globalization:** 3 billion new capitalists willing to do a lot more for a lot less
- **Divergent offerings:** disruptive new technologies that eliminate traditional ways of doing jobs—and, occasionally, entire industries

Many of these disruptions are new phenomena, their full fury yet to be felt. Individually, any one of these new realities can dramatically shorten the life cycle of an offering. In combination, they can be as devastating as any Level 5 hurricane—threatening the long-term survival of the organization itself.

This is forcing all executives to rethink their strategies on two fronts: where to make the significant investments *today* to guarantee a successful *future* (differentiation), without sacrificing the short-term results necessary to satisfy all stakeholders (productivity). With C-suite turnover at an all-time high in 2008, be assured that highly compensated executives take this challenge very seriously. And, it doesn't require a leap of imagination—or an expensive consulting study—to understand that organizational sustainability—consistent, profitable growth—suffers when C-level turnover is on the rise.

EXERCISE

How are the new realities described in this section affecting your ability to grow sales? Which have had the most impact? Do you think this disruption will get worse—or is it just temporary?

Now I want you to put on a different hat. After completing this first part, try and put yourself in the shoes of your best customers. Which of the new realities are negatively impacting their abilities to grow their businesses? If you're not sure, how might you find out? Do you think your customers might be looking for help in this area?

Challenges to Greatness

The book *Good to Great*, by Jim Collins, is essentially about those few organizations that are able to grow profitably for at least two decades. One of the most difficult elements of his research, Collins lamented, was finding good companies to study.

Organizations that had demonstrated the ability to deliver consistent, profitable growth for more than twenty years were in short supply.

One reason why companies have such difficulty sustaining profitable growth lies in Joseph Schumpeter's well-known theory of "Creative Destruction"—not a new phenomenon at all. What makes markets perfect, Schumpeter argued, is that large profits attract competition. Competition drives down prices and margins, effectively commoditizing offerings that were once atypical. For instance, around the turn of the twentieth century, there were essentially two car manufacturers—Ford and Alfred Sloan's General Motors. Choices for buyers were limited ("I'll build any color car as long as it is black" was Henry Ford's famous comment on consumer choice). Today, not only has choice exploded (domestic auto manufacturers have too many brands to mention) but also global competition has swelled, causing a low-margin, oversupply situation that will predictably lead to once seemingly invincible auto manufacturers going out of business. This is not a question of if, but when.

This is the predictable nature of markets. But Schumpeter's theory of economic Darwinism doesn't account for the new *speed* at which products, profit margins, and *companies* now decay. Sustaining profitable growth is an entirely different challenge when product and service life cycles have been reduced from years to months.

Look no further than the everyday cell phone to illustrate this point. In the "olden" days of wireless telephony (a decade ago), the life cycle of a cell phone was twelve to fourteen months. This meant that Motorola, NEC, and Samsung could generate almost a full year of profits from a product line before significant reengineering was required. Today, with the new convergent capabilities of audio, video, and text, a new category of cell phone seems to be introduced almost weekly. This rapid innovation reality has collapsed the birth-to-death life cycle of a cell phone to barely a few months.

This new reality is being experienced in industry after industry. Innovation is not linear or constant. In fact, technological advancement is exponential in nature, enabling consistently faster cycles of innovation. Simultaneously, organizational ability to absorb and adapt to radically new ways of doing work is also accelerating.

Many decades ago, I was told that "one major change a year" was all an individual should attempt. This one change was considered a sort of biological maximum not to be violated. Not anymore. New generations of young workers have thrown the prevailing wisdom that people are resistant to change out the window. In fact, it's the reverse—a sort of evolutionary reality that contributes to the further acceleration and collapse of product life cycles. As we are presented with new options at a faster and faster rate, we demand new options at a faster and faster rate.

The point is that the new reality of innovation—both creation by competitors and adaptation by markets—is applying tremendous strain on senior executives who are in a constant state of retooling the future, having to make big-bet decisions about the future that often come down to nothing more than a hunch.

This is the blessing and curse of the new realities just described. For customer executives, opportunities may be greater than ever—but the window in which to make money is shorter. This is the paradox faced by senior executives excited by the new world of opportunity but simultaneously threatened by the realization that core offerings are quickly exposed to the ravages of commoditization.

The end game is that customer executives have been forced to look to nontraditional areas for help. Customers are now collaborating with vendors as never before, understanding that cheaper-better-faster products and services are not the only places where real, impactful value can be mined.

And, how did MasterCard eventually fare in its pursuit to deliver more *strategic* value to customers? "Connecting to client strategy didn't just open doors—it blasted them open," said Michael Lazarus, the former vice president of customer strategy for MasterCard. "We began doing some very different things with customers—facilitating their strategic planning sessions, getting involved in customer operations, and helping the client with nontraditional marketing. Not only did we gain a seat at the table, but, in many instances, the business totally flipped from being a distant second in the account to being number one in a short period of time."

BUYING NEEDS NO SALESPEOPLE

Let me illustrate the power of connecting to customer strategy by understanding a customer's internal and external decision drivers with another case study. This particular case study well illustrates how new realities are rapidly changing the game for all salespeople.

Wal-Mart needs no introduction. Its relentless focus on "everyday low costs" has created a culture of no-nonsense, no-frills, and, recently, no salespeople. A few years back, Wal-Mart commissioned a study of its procurement practices. Wal-Mart was spending hundreds of millions of dollars of valuable resource spend in procurement and was looking for ways to improve productivity. In traipsed the consultants. After months of study, Wal-Mart executives gleaned two critical pieces of information:

1. The average procurement person saw 6.8 salespeople per day.

2. The 3,800 procurement personnel were spending the majority of their time procuring low-margin products that contributed to only a small percentage of Wal-Mart profits.

Based on these data, what strategic changes would you make to procurement practices if you were the CEO of Wal-Mart?

Wal-Mart's approach shook the sales profession to its core. The company asked, What value did our procurement people gain by visiting with all these vendor salespeople? In other words, were these meetings even necessary?

The answer? No. Wal-Mart decided that procurement people were far better off not meeting with salespeople. Today, procurement people spend far more time using the Internet as a buying, vendor sourcing, and negotiation mechanism, adding a whole new dimension of efficiency to an already savvy procurement process. And the results have been extraordinary in a number of different ways.

First, buying through the Web enabled Wal-Mart to drastically reduce the number of procurement people—by almost half—saving hundreds of millions of dollars. Furthermore, the Internet allowed the company to purchase products at cheaper prices—a savings it could pass on to its customers. "Don't call on us—we'll call on you," was the new message sent to vendors. "And when we do call, it will probably be through the Internet." The implication for vendors—now that you won't be paying sales commissions anymore, you can drop your prices even further.

The herd is being thinned.

And this new reality is just in its incubation phase. Shortly after Wal-Mart enacted its new procurement processes, a large manufacturer followed suit, trimming its procurement department from twelve hundred people to four hundred people. This move gave it the productivity gain of better procurement with fewer people. And productivity is king, its only competitor for the limelight being differentiation.

The Wal-Mart case study illustrates the new, relentless drive by organizations to buy as cost-efficiently as possible—sales relationships be damned! And today, a new breed of procurement people have been tasked to do just that. Salespeople are learning that there's a new sheriff in town—supply chain management. These new teams are equipped with a new set of tools to make sure the job of price reduction gets done fast and right. The consequences to organizations and salespeople who ignore this shift and continue to compete on product value alone will be grave.

You might be asking whether a salesperson stands a chance under such circumstances? How does one become strategically valuable when a customer is so intent on buying products at the cheapest price?

I think you will agree that, given Wal-Mart's trends in procurement and pricing, if a vendor could break through those barriers and actually become strategically indispensable to Wal-Mart, the possibility exists for any salesperson or vendor to also become strategically indispensable to their customers.

Well, it's possible. Back when the new realities of procurement were just emerging, forward-thinking leadership at P&G foresaw these trends. Led by Tom Muccio, their vice president in charge of the Wal-Mart account, they began examining different ways to impact Wal-Mart beyond just their product brands. Just read the following case study, and you'll learn how P&G became more strategically valuable by teaching its sales team to go down a nontraditional path.

Becoming Strategically Valuable

Procter & Gamble, an organization in the ultimate commodity business, sells soap and shampoo—mature categories that face intense global competition. As I've discussed, selling commodity products in a transparent and standardized global economy is an unforgiving challenge. Remember, new realities are forcing traditional product companies to rethink the type of value they must offer customers—and whether salespeople need to play a different role in the process of how customer value is created and captured.

Tom Muccio was the vice president of sales for P&G in the days when Wal-Mart emerged from being an unknown entity to becoming a retail powerhouse. Though P&G was doing a tremendous amount of business with Wal-Mart, Muccio knew his company was just scratching the surface. Muccio understood that in order to do more with Wal-Mart, P&G would have to add more value to Wal-Mart's strategy. This was a different mind-set—one that went against the grain of the traditional "sell something to someone" P&G sales culture.

To shake up his sales and account management team, Muccio created the bold goal of growing P&G's business with Wal-Mart at a faster rate than Wal-Mart's actual growth pace. In the mid-to-late '80s, when Wal-Mart was expanding at meteoric rates, this was no easy feat.

Muccio observed that there were three different cycles in which P&G sellers engaged with Wal-Mart people. The first cycle was the operations cycle, when sellers discussed the products that P&G needed to supply to Wal-Mart in the short run. The second cycle was the financial cycle, during which sellers focused on the next eighteen months to ensure that newly constructed Wal-Mart stores would be adequately supplied. The last cycle was where Muccio felt P&G could be most customer relevant. This was the innovation cycle, the one where P&G salespeople and Wal-Mart executives met to converse about the future.

What happened in these sessions? Let's first note what *didn't* happen. There were absolutely no product demonstrations or pitches. In other words, Muccio and his team made *no attempts* to sell products during any of the sessions. Instead, there was a lot of brainstorming, listening, debating, and collaborative discussion. Questions would often start with "what if?" Topics could be highly varied, but most focused on establishing where Wal-Mart wanted to be in the future and how P&G could help the company reach its goals. The following are examples of the questions that were discussed during the sessions.

- What new market segments should Wal-Mart pursue in the future?
- Which marketing methods could P&G teach Wal-Mart that might help Wal-Mart attract better talent?
- What new product categories might P&G create exclusively for Wal-Mart that would separate them from anticipated competitors?
- How could P&G help Wal-Mart achieve better SKU results?

As the questions suggest, the discussions focused on establishing a joint vision and problem-solving process, information sharing, and generally moving away from the "lowest common denominator" pricing issues that had previously defined the relationship between Wal-Mart and P&G. Though price was important, Muccio and his team weren't discussing the price of a bar of soap or whether they could cut a penny or two from the price of a bottle of shampoo. Everyone understood that P&G had to meet certain price and operational parameters if the company was going to do business with Wal-Mart.

In Muccio's words, "In reality the cheapest price wasn't where Wal-Mart executives saw the most value." It was the ability to create new forms of value—particularly through the innovation cycle—that most distinguished P&G from its competitors. Wal-Mart quickly understood that P&G's focus was simply on helping—not selling. It was during these sessions that both companies became one team. They were on the same side of the table.

The results? From 1987, when Tom Muccio initiated the changes, to 2003, shortly before his retirement, P&G's sales to Wal-Mart grew from $350 million to $7.8 billion. That's B as in *billion*.

BUILD A VALUE PIPELINE

Ultimately, Tom Muccio and his team created a very large and flexible pipe between Wal-Mart and P&G through which nontraditional value could flow. This portal was not built overnight—it was a trial-and-error process. There were occasional leaks that needed to be fixed—no relationship is without challenges. And preventing conversations from declining to the lowest common denominator (cheaper price) was a constant challenge.

But this pipeline was built sufficiently strong to shield the strategic value flow from succumbing to politics, power, or the individual needs of any one department. The philosophy was that the greater good must prevail.

Prior to constructing this pipeline, the two companies were essentially connected via dozens of different smaller pipes. The business units of P&G were myopically focused on selling their products and hitting their sales targets, but they were ignoring the opportunity for a bigger win for both organizations. There were a few hooks connected to a few loops, but a strong, secure, and complete connection was lacking. Ultimately, this new partnership enabled the discovery of large amounts of "hidden" money that could be mined by Muccio's team—hard dollars that could be saved from the inefficiencies of a classic vendor/customer relationship. Tom Muccio and Wal-Mart would tap this hidden money time and again, validating the economic value of the relationship to both entities. The connection grew stronger and stronger as more loops and more hooks came into play.

Is there a lesson here for salespeople? From our perspective, almost eight billion lessons, although I'll boil it down to a few caveats: challenge tradition, quit selling, and begin helping. In other words, focus on understanding, connecting, and adding value to customer strategy.

Tom Muccio took the time to learn the strategy of Wal-Mart. This meant learning the Wal-Mart master plan, the unique value they delivered to customers, their processes, and their strategies—no easy feat when representing a traditional product-centric company so intensely focused on getting the customer to stock more product. He abandoned some of the well-worn, traditional sales methodologies that P&G had clung to for decades. And, by staying focused on adding value to a bigger picture beyond tactical products, he transcended the role of salesperson. He became a customer confidant—a trusted advisor. He created Velcro value and earned a seat at the table.

Different Sells

As it turns out, the best way to differentiate yourself from the competition is to help your clients differentiate from theirs! Fairfield Manufacturing is a case in point. In early 2000, the Lafayette, Indiana–based manufacturer of gears was fighting for its very survival. Low-cost global competitors had entered the fray, and the market had softened. As a result, revenues fell drastically, and the company was hemorrhaging cash. For this proud company, the outlook was bleak.

Enter Paul Schleuter, the new vice president of sales, and his differentiation mind-set. Schleuter's theory was that gearing components and products—the two traditional revenue sources for Fairfield—needed a value face-lift. He felt that something he called "systems solutions" was the type of value customers just might be looking for. A systems solution would help a client differentiate their products—an area where Fairfield customers often needed help.

Schleuter felt systems solutions was a game changer. The goal was not only to elevate revenues and margins but also to improve the company's reputation. This would require a sales force that engaged different people in different conversations, and JLG, a small customer, presented such an opportunity.

JLG is a manufacturer of large mobile equipment, such as cranes and lift trucks. Although a small customer, the relationship had all the hallmarks of the "old way" of business, with lowest price often determining vendor preference. Then the opportunity occurred.

On a sales call to JLG, Fairfield learned that JLG was considering getting out of the scissor lift business. Rising warranty costs and new, cheaper global competitors were putting enormous pressure on profitability. Senior level executives at JLG had a big decision to make—and it appeared a certainty that the company would soon stop manufacturing scissor lifts.

Schleuter suggested to JLG senior executives that they conduct a collaborative session focused on how Fairfield could create new forms of value, specifically through technology, for JLG and help them define their strategy. These collaborations—something new to Fairfield—would include a mix of Fairfield and JLG key personnel from multiple departments. The purpose of these ideation sessions was threefold:

1. Learn JLG strategy, specifically the core business drivers. Although Fairfield had been selling to JLG for years, the company did not truly understand the corporate strategy that drove important decisions. *It was time to find out.*

2. Assess whether Fairfield could add value to JLG, specifically by helping JLG create a new, *differentiated* scissor lift line that would disrupt competitors and put JLG back on the map.

3. Educate JLG on potential new enabling technologies, technologies that might help JLG create a new line of scissor lift trucks radically different from current models.

The game changed for both companies as a result of a new type of relationship. Schleuter's team was able to see JLG from a strategic perspective, a very different perspective from one focused on moving gearing components and products. "This might seem like common sense, but we've been in the products business so long that it doesn't dawn on many of our salespeople to have these discussions," commented Schleuter. "These sessions were a mechanism that put us on the same side of the table as the customer—a real first for us."

The half-day collaborations began with questioning, listening, and learning about general JLG business issues, such as market potential, profitability, distribution, positioning, and lifetime value. "Some very strong bonds developed—we were mutually dependent to make this work. And, ultimately, it led to what both companies were hoping for—a radical reinvention of the scissor lift line that ultimately led to a real market breakthrough for JLG."

The result was that JLG committed to developing a radically different scissor lift line, which today is an incredibly successful and profitable line. Fairfield is now considered a *partner* with JLG, doing many times more business now than in its previous relationship. Fairfield gained a "seat" at JLG's table.

Using the JLG experience as a model, the Fairfield sales team has taken many of their customer relationships to a whole new level. Fairfield invested in training salespeople how to sell systems solutions, and now its salespeople are vastly better at learning client strategy. A foreign concept for many of their salespeople just a few years back, learning client strategy is a real breakthrough in how Fairfield now does business.

As for the impact on profit margins, Schleuter suggested looking at the margins to determine whether a salesperson has shifted to a differentiation mind-set. "If you're a product salesperson, your margins are getting squeezed. Conversely, if you're a businessperson helping clients differentiate, your gross profit margins are vastly superior. And, I'm not just talking about a few points—it is a very noticeable gap."

Understanding that profit margins are the key, Schleuter believes Fairfield's margins are simply a reflection of the value the company adds to customers. "The client always rewards you based on value—a bitter truth for some organizations experiencing flat sales and margin erosion. When this happens, customers are indirectly telling you something: 'you aren't making much impact anymore.' But, as we've learned, this message just means that they still need all kinds of help—just in nontraditional places, in areas where salespeople aren't necessarily used to looking."

THE BASIC RULES

Let's face it: If you are trying to change your selling approach, you're probably doing it for one or both of the following reasons. First, you are passionate about your business and helping your customers. Second, you want to grow sales—the money part. To accomplish both—selling more by helping more—will require more influence on spend decisions so that you get bigger portions of customers' budgets for longer periods of time. It's that simple. And to make that happen, we have to connect to strategy.

But before you learn your customer's strategy, you'll need to learn a few rules to help you understand how connecting to strategy will result in greater sales.

Rule #1:   Strategy dictates spend.

Rule #2:   To change spend, add value to customer strategy.

Let me explain these two important rules. Any organization is simply a chain of command. Strategy is created at senior levels, communicated throughout, and then driven downward, with a focus on accountability. In fact, most people in organizations ultimately serve as implementers, executing strategies made by others at more senior levels. Budgets are then debated and enacted based on these strategies. If you want to learn why a company budgets as they do, simply take some time to learn their strategy. In other words, when the code of strategy is cracked—something you will learn to do in this book—it becomes apparent why the organization spends money the way it does. And that is when you will understand how to connect in a way that will earn you a seat at the table.

BE LIKE VELCRO

Smart executives understand that the game has changed. The real treasure for customers now lies in previously unmined places of value. Product value has been trumped. Value has gone upstream, and the companies that paddle to this part of the river will have the advantage.

Remember, all the customer cares about is value. Yet the traditional product value that salespeople have always delivered is no longer as important in a transparent, standardized, and global economy. The paradox is that salespeople are needed more than ever—but only if they learn to connect to their customers in new ways.

You need to "be like Velcro"—in how you connect your solutions to client challenges and how you connect your value to client strategies. When you enter this realm of connection, you no longer compete, but create. And your customers will pay you accordingly.

CHAPTER FOUR

BRIDGING THE DIVIDE

Creating demand with senior executives was truly a different game. We mentally had to get out of the *products* business and into the *results* business. When this finally happened, everything changed—from who we called on, to what we discussed. To create demand, we had to sell change, and that required us to change.

—Tom Muccio, former president of global consumer teams, Procter & Gamble

I'VE SAID IT BEFORE AND I'LL SAY IT AGAIN: the skills to sell and create demand for complex solutions are very different from those required to sell mature, core products and services. The differences are especially pronounced when your divergent offerings are new in the industry. This requires transcending the mid-level and calling on the C-suite—a whole new game for most salespeople. For example, let's compare the games of poker and craps. There are a few similarities—both are wagering games played in a casino—but they are very different games. And if you're going on a four-day spree to Las Vegas with a big stash of cash hoping to turn it into an even bigger stash, you'll want to pay close attention to this distinction to maximize your chances of success.

A DIVERGENT VIEW

In *The Innovators Solution*, one of the better business books of the last decade, author Clayton Christensen advised readers to "Think of products as things people hire to do a job." The idea that products and services are things that people hire is an especially useful perspective for any salesperson wishing to better align with the mind-set of the buyer.

In this context, the biggest challenge buyers face is determining whether they should "hire" solutions that offer radically different ways of getting work done or achieving certain objectives. Radical solutions can offer huge upsides, but the pain and risk of adoption can be significant. And there are always—always— safer bets out there, at least from the buyer's perspective.

A few decades back, research proved that not all sales are created equal. The framework required to sell large, complex offerings was entirely different from that required to sell small, low-risk products and services. Today, a new model has emerged. This model recognizes that there are two types of solutions available to any customer—a critical distinction for a salesperson to understand if one's goal is to influence client decisions. (See figure 4.1.) The model categorizes large sales into two types:

- **Concurrent offerings:** Products and services that are consistent with the way a job is currently done by an individual or organization, intended to offer marginal value gain to the customer
- **Divergent offerings:** Solutions that represent radically new or different ways of getting a job done, often requiring significant customer change to net immensely better results

FIGURE 4.1: THE UNIQUE CHALLENGE OF SELLING DIVERGENT OFFERINGS

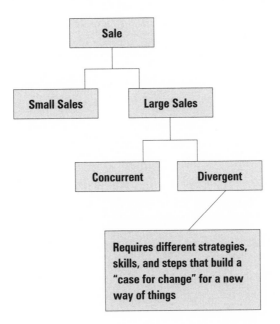

For forward thinking organizations tasked with selling "new-to-the-world" solutions, this distinction is critical if opportunities—the seeds of all growth—are to be managed effectively. To better understand the distinction, let's take the simple example of someone who wants to watch a movie in the comfort of their own home. For the last two decades the concurrent—or traditional—method of obtaining the movie was to rent it at Blockbuster or some other brick-and-mortar store. Then Netflix came along. Netflix offered a divergent way of obtaining a movie to watch in your home. With Netflix, you no longer needed to stand in line, absorb a late fee, or worry whether or not your favorite movie would be in stock. Netflix was a divergent offering that has proved disruptive to the traditional way of business as usual, as evidenced by the continued slide of Blockbuster stock.

By combining three simple elements—the DVD, postal delivery, and the Web—a divergent offering was born, *a fundamentally new way of getting a job done.*

Most organizations today have become surprisingly proficient at creating divergent offerings. These are often companies that have combined or leveraged technology with their traditional offerings to create radically new ways of getting jobs done. For these organizations, the goal is always the same—to swim in a new pool of faster growth and premium profit margins.

For salespeople, selling an offering that is divergent or high risk is truly a different game, and it requires a conscious understanding that a different selling approach will be required. Figure 4.2 highlights the differences between divergent and concurrent offerings from a seller's perspective, differences that are explored in detail throughout the book.

FIGURE 4.2: DIVERGENT OFFERINGS: A DIFFERENT SELLING CHALLENGE

	Concurrent Offerings	Divergent Offerings
Real Enemy?	Traditional competition	"No decision"
Who to Call On?	Mid-level managers	Senior executives
Conversations?	Pain focused	Opportunity focused
Value Proposition?	Product value	Strategic value
Why Buyers Change?	Cheaper-better-faster products and services	Enables differentiation and/or productivity gains that are aligned with core strategies

EXERCISE

What distinguishes a divergent offering from one that is concurrent? The customer's perspective. What one customer might consider divergent and risky, another progressive company from the same industry might consider mainstream and low risk. So, from the only perspective that really matters—the customer's—how would you categorize your solutions? Does this distinction change not only who you must sell to but also how you must sell?

CURIOSITY AND COMMITMENT

The good news is that executives are often curious about new ways of doing things, especially when those changes can have a radical impact on the bottom line. Curiosity and commitment are two entirely different things, though.

The executives you call on are smart people. They understand the significant "change costs" associated with the successful adoption of new, complex, divergent solutions. They understand that real change happens in the trenches, not in executive offices or boardrooms. Big change will require employees to think and act differently. The upside may be big, but the downside is significant as well.

One cannot underscore the difficulty inherent in selling divergent or complex offerings, especially in scenarios where demand must be created. A wonderful vignette on the difficulty of change comes from Machiavelli's *The Prince*. This passage was suggested by our friend David Charlton, a senior executive with Corning, which is considered one of the most innovative companies in the world. Corning executives know a thing or two about how difficult it can be to convince customers to implement a new order of things.

> There is nothing . . . more doubtful of success than an
> attempt to introduce a new order of things . . . The inno-
> vator has for enemies all those who derived advantages
> from the old order of things, while those who expect to
> benefit by the new order will be but lukewarm defenders.
> This indifference arises in part from fear of their adver-
> saries . . . and partly from the incredulity of established
> experience.

This brilliant prose explains why true change masters carefully herd together all those in a decision base. They understand that solutions requiring big change call for unanimity among many decision makers. In other words, serious change that requires major commitment will necessitate building bridges that take executives beyond mere curiosity and that eliminate the divide between adversaries and supporters of the new order.

We call this process "bridging the divide"—a process that requires salespeople to build a bedrock foundation for change—with change-resistant organizations. To do this requires a sound knowledge of an organization's master strategies (the subject of the next chapter) and a different FOCAS (an executive connection technique I'll describe in chapter 7).

Divergent Offering

Trimble is a good example of a traditional company that leveraged technology to create a divergent offering. For many decades, Trimble has been a leader in the surveying market, manufacturing the traditional optical equipment you often see surveyors using in large road construction projects. Remember the last time you were twenty minutes late for an appointment because of a traffic jam due to road construction? There is a good chance that Trimble equipment was used in the bottleneck construction area that caused your cursing.

Eventually, lower-priced global competitors emerged that forced Trimble to trim pricing on its core surveying equipment products. As average prices dropped from $3,000 to $1,500, salespeople needed to sell twice as many units just to keep pace with the previous year's revenue level. Trimble leaders knew they needed to differentiate in a big way if it was to counter slower growth and waning profits.

And innovate they did! Trimble introduced a new technology to its construction customers—GPS satellite technology. In the past, a construction company needed to hire surveyors to stake out a construction site before a bulldozer could do its work—an expensive, slow, and laborious process. GPS enabled contractors to install new technology on their bulldozers that would automatically raise and lower the blade without the need of an operator. As it pushed dirt, the dozer automatically conformed to pre-plotted survey data that synchronized with a satellite in the sky.

The success of this new technology—eventually—exceeded even the most optimistic of forecasts. Today, construction companies need not depend on any third party to do the job of moving dirt, allowing work to be done at a much lower cost. Not only did road construction productivity improve, but this technology also significantly differentiated construction companies that were early adopters.

The technology even had residual benefits. Fewer traffic jams meant reduced motorist frustration, minimizing road rage that potentially prevented the spiritually inclined from meeting their maker. Disruptive technologies, like a higher authority, can work in funny ways, too. I'm not sure whether Trimble technology was ever approved by the church, but it had a big impact on both Trimble revenues and contractor customer profits.

Yet selling this complex solution was not without its challenges early on. In its infancy, there was little demand for this new technology. Executives were curious, but at the steep price of over $100,000 to outfit one bulldozer, they were a long way from committed. And prospects weren't the only ones with sticker shock. The Trimble and dealer salespeople used to selling $1,500 products to mid-level managers had little idea how to sell six-figure solutions to senior executives of construction companies.

How did they transition from selling tactical products to selling business solutions? We began working with Trimble soon after this new technology emerged. Leadership saw a huge opportunity to vault ahead of the competition, but they were frustrated at the inability of the sales team to gain customer traction for the new technology. The company was ready to deploy the differentiated technology. Its salespeople needed to get traction quickly, before new competitors emerged. The stakes were high, so we began by helping sales leadership understand that selling divergent technology requires a different selling framework for one very simple reason: selling divergent offerings is a *whole new game.*

SELLING CHANGE REQUIRES CHANGE

Trimble represents an excellent example of why selling divergent solutions requires a different market-facing approach. Selling $100,000 GPS systems is an entirely different challenge from selling mainstream $1,500 survey instruments—the previously accepted norm for "how a job was done." It's easy to see how the selling differences between divergent and concurrent offerings outlined at the beginning of this chapter presented real challenges for Trimble.

- Early on, there was no demand for GPS systems. Salespeople needed to create demand.
- Trimble was very early to market, attempting to gain first-mover advantage. That meant that the real enemy to success was not traditional competition but "no decision." The prospect refrain of "we're going to wait until next year" was a more powerful enemy than any external competitor.

- Selling GPS required salespeople to have business conversations with senior level construction company executives. Product presentations did not resonate with senior executives who did not care about the nuances of a new technology. Rather, senior executive prospects wondered whether this technology warranted a change in their strategy, something an elaborate presentation could not answer. (I'll address how to tackle this challenge in the next chapter.)
- Product conversations were about "pain"—the need for cheaper-better-faster surveying instruments. Business conversations were about results—applying technology to *differentiate from* and *disrupt* slower-moving competitors. Effectively done, this was a discussion as much about future opportunity as it was current productivity.

Ultimately, Trimble elected to do something nontraditional: train salespeople how to connect and add value to customer strategy. This approach went far beyond the superficial return on investment and value-calculator selling strategies that had failed to gain traction in the past.

Martin Trudelle, a former sales director at Trimble, commented on how the sales team needed to change before the company could realize success:

> Before, we were trying to apply our old "strategic selling" methodologies to each GPS opportunity. Our past training taught salespeople *what* to do, but not *how* to do it—something we identified as a critical gap in our sales education. In other words, it was helpful knowing whether someone was an economic buyer, user buyer, or champion, but that didn't tell us *how* to execute sales calls with senior executives. Our presentations were gaining interest, but not closure.

What turned it around for us was seeing that selling a divergent offering would require a different sales process. This was a new sandbox—at least, new sand. And playing would require Trimble and distributor salespeople to have the type of business conversations that could ultimately stimulate demand with the executives on whom we were calling.

As a result of training its sales force on how to build a case for change and create demand for divergent technology, customer adoption rates accelerated. The end result was that Trimble dominated the construction market, thus driving the growth of the enterprise. But the key was in understanding that demand creation was the key competence that salespeople needed to learn before new, divergent offerings would be accepted by customers.

SET SAIL

The first step in improving selling effectiveness lies in understanding that "not all sales are created equal." This is especially true for those faced with selling divergent, complex offerings that customer executives perceive as high reward, but equally high risk. In these cases, demand is best created by attaching the offering to a ship that already set sail—that vessel being customer strategy.

In other words, average salespeople often attempt to sell a divergent offering on its inherent benefits. This often involves tying the value proposition to the pain points of the customer. This strategy inherently lacks the muscle to get the job of customer adoption done. Espousing benefits and uncovering problems may create curiosity, but it rarely generates customer commitment to a new order of things.

Businesspeople who sell are far wiser. Instead of selling isolated value, they attach their value proposition to something that already has momentum—specifically the master strategic plans of their clients. We'll learn about these oceans in our next chapter. By attaching to these two strategic imperatives, a seaworthy vessel is constructed that will carry your value proposition through new, uncharted, and often turbulent waters.

Are you ready for this dispatch? You're about to travel into new territory, full of dangerous Red Ocean sharks and exciting Blue Ocean treasures.

CHAPTER FIVE

THE GREAT GAME OF STRATEGY

I see a lot of salespeople put pressure on customers to close deals. We're more interested that our salespeople patiently nurture relationships. And, when you are patient on purpose, clients appreciate it. When they see that you are genuinely trying to help, they start thinking, "these guys get it." Then they not only *want to work* with you, they actually look for ways to do business with you.

—Kim Purcell, managing director, O.C. Tanner

ENVISION THAT YOU ARE FLYING TO VEGAS on a private corporate jet with the senior executive team of a large customer. You were invited to come along due to your expertise in gambling. This is going to be a high-stakes weekend, and your clients are open to anything that can improve their odds of winning.

The table game these executives have chosen is craps. As in any other game, there are a great many philosophies about the best way to win. Different players can have wildly different strategies. Some players are extremely conservative with their chips, feeling that a grind-it-out strategy is the best course. Other players are risk takers. When they feel the timing is right, they pounce—often betting all their chips in an all-or-nothing gambit.

I am an awful craps player, but some of my friends are very, very good at craps. When I'm with them at the tables in Vegas, they always want me to play. But I know that if I do I'm going to lose for one simple reason—I don't understand how the game is *really* played. I know a few rules, a few of the ins and outs, but nothing in-depth that would give me an edge.

In other words, you can't even begin to think about advising someone else on winning if you don't understand the *real* rules of the game. If you do, our aforementioned executives will be inclined to leave you in Vegas with no ride home because your advice was useless. This will only make your life *more* miserable as your significant other will be very unhappy with the ridiculous money you lost trying to play a game you didn't understand in the first place.

The purpose of this chapter is to teach you how the great game of corporate strategy is played. Once you learn the rules, you can begin having intelligent discussions with those actively engaged in the game. Knowing the rules gives you important common ground—an important building block in developing relationships with senior executives who are typically resistant to taking advice from traditional salespeople.

A PLAN FOR UNDERSTANDING STRATEGY

Strategy is pretty simple stuff—as long as you have the proper schema to act as a road map. A schema is a mental model that serves as a visual reference point. For example, a blueprint of a new home is a schema. Schemas help you quickly make sense of a complicated situation, essentially helping you reach—in the words of Oliver Wendell Holmes—the simplicity on the other side of complexity.

The schema I'm going to give you is a one-page visual reference that will help you understand the master strategic plan of an organization. In its simplest form, it will help you understand how an organization intends to sustainably make money. This schema will serve as a filter in your conversations with executives, helping you better understand their historical decisions and current thinking. It will also help you understand why and where they have placed their bets.

If you were talking to your builder about making a few construction changes, a blueprint would anchor your conversations, serving as a reference point to make intelligent decisions. Like a good blueprint, this strategic schema will keep your conversations tight, relevant, and soundly rooted.

The schema that I've created is based on two distinct schools of thought about strategy and decision making. The first is the concept of Blue Ocean and Red Ocean strategies, developed by W. Chan Kim and Renée Mauborgne in their popular business book *Blue Ocean Strategy* (Harvard Business School Press, 2005), a treatise on how to create new forms of customer value. The second is an analysis of the two types of decisions high-level executives make almost every day that dictate how they allocate funds: important decisions and urgent decisions. This distinction was made by Geoffrey A. Moore, author of many books on marketing, in his book *Dealing with Darwin: How Great Companies Innovate at Every Phase of Their Evolution* (Portfolio, 2005).

Before I present the schema (the Master Strategic Plan Matrix on page 63), though, I will explain these significant concepts, beginning with Blue and Red Oceans.

OCEANS TWO

The first component of the schema is represented by two very large oceans—one red and the other blue. Each ocean represents a different category of strategy, each diametrically opposed.

A Red Ocean strategy is any strategy that supports the "core business" of the enterprise. This is the domain of mature, competitive categories—products, services, or markets on which a company has relied for past growth and profits. Unfortunately, competition has gradually swooped in and commoditized offerings that were once new and unique. These competitive realities make profitable growth especially difficult. In the Red Ccean, markets have matured, growth has slowed, and Schumpeter's Creative Destruction (described earlier) is in full force. Remember the two strategy drivers—productivity and differentiation? Well, productivity objectives fall primarily in the Red Ocean.

A Blue Ocean strategy is any strategy that supports the new products, services, or markets that represent higher margins and faster growth. This is the place where the company sees its best opportunities for future growth. The goal in this space is to separate from the competitive herd through significant differentiation. Moving from a "product excellence" strategy to a "total solutions" strategy would be an example of a Blue Ocean play. Big bets are made here—often pure investment requiring a huge leap of faith (hey, you have to believe in something, right?).

In *Blue Ocean Strategy*, the authors use the circus industry as a way to contrast the two oceans. Red Ocean is the traditional three-ring circus saddled with high-overhead animals—a marginalized, no growth, dying industry. Blue Ocean is Cirque du Soleil—a surreal drama set to music and performed in sold-out theaters at over $100 per seat.

Not unlike two growing teenage boys, both the Blue and Red Oceans have endless appetites, as I mentioned when discussing productivity and differentiation. Thus, the budget wars fought in the last quarter of every fiscal year—intense battles among managers for the scarce resources of the enterprise needed to feed the strategies of their functional departments or divisions.

The Psychology of Blue and Red Spend

This simple categorization of strategy into Blue or Red Ocean explains the senior executive psychology around wagering resources. In effect, when a company spends a dollar, it is doing it for either differentiation (Blue Ocean) or productivity (Red Ocean) reasons. From the senior executive perch, underfeeding the Blue Ocean will lead to the long-term demise of the organization. In other words, lack of investment in research and development or innovation will surely kill the golden goose. In this case, differentiation will suffer. Conversely, underfunding the Red Ocean may hurt the ability to compete in the short term. It takes money to keep the cash cow consistently pumping revenues. Lack of investment in Red Ocean people and systems might hurt the short-term quarterly numbers—a definite no-no to senior executives driven to succeed (and maintain their own employment). In this case, productivity will suffer.

For example, Sogistics, the company I founded twenty years ago, does "sales productivity" work with sales teams in need of transformation. Training salespeople is usually an important component of these projects. You might think that the motivation behind a customer investment in training is always the same—better sales. Actually, the executive motivation behind such an investment is as different as night and day (or, in this case, Red and Blue).

For instance, we often hear from sales executives who are frustrated with the inability of their sales teams to sell traditional offerings to mature markets. They typically request sales training on how to call higher, close better, or negotiate with the procurement folks who are putting so much price pressure on them. In these cases, any dollar expended on sales training would be spent for Red Ocean reasons.

Let's look at the other extreme, citing O.C. Tanner, our extended case study. As you recall, O.C. Tanner is a market leader in the long-term service award industry, with about $350 million in revenues. Over the years, competition increased, commoditizing previously profitable products. Their category had also drawn the attention of customer procurement departments interested in gaining a significant price decrease through the typical RFP process. The company, led by CEO Kent Murdoch, had created a bold differentiation strategy (total recognition solutions) that would require salespeople to sell at least two or three levels "up"—to chief human resource directors, divisional heads, and the C-suite—as a means to sustain the growth of the enterprise.

John McVeigh, senior vice president of global sales, made a decision to hire my firm, Sogistics, to help with this effort. Our focus was on layering a new set of competencies onto the sales team that would enable them to connect their new solution sets to the core strategies of customers. In this case, every dollar and every resource spent in training the sales and account management teams was spent for Blue Ocean reasons.

From the O.C. Tanner perspective, they had a new differentiation strategy. The window of opportunity was open. But getting through this window in a short period of time would not be accomplished unless salespeople learned to think and act very differently from how they had in the past. This was a classic Blue Ocean differentiation spend. And as we'll soon learn, senior executives do not "weight" these two spends equally, often seeing significantly more value in a Blue Ocean expenditure than a Red Ocean expenditure.

Blended Spend

To better understand this concept of categorizing spend as either Red or Blue Ocean, you need look no further than your own place of work. When your company invested in a new information technology system, launched a new marketing initiative, or hired that key new person in your department, was it for Blue or Red Ocean reasons?

Take this book for example. Did you spend the $20 to help you sell traditional products or services—your personal Red Ocean? Or did you invest because you have exciting new Blue Ocean opportunities—new offerings and/or new markets—that you need to take advantage of quickly?

If you had difficulty answering either of these questions, perhaps it's due to the fact that expenditures are often blended. In other words, the investment was meant to impact *both* the Blue and Red Oceans. Take the new sales associate your company hired last year as an example. He may spend the majority of time calling on traditional markets and selling traditional products. But part of his job is to sell in a completely new market for your company, and the vice president of sales has instructed him to spend 25 percent of selling time here. In this case, 75 cents of every dollar invested in Pat goes into the Red Ocean bucket, and 25 cents goes into the Blue bucket.

URGENT—OR IMPORTANT?

In *Dealing with Darwin* Geoffrey Moore discusses how senior executives attempt to sustain growth. Along the way, he describes how resource-allocation decisions are made—always a controversial process full of debate, second-guessing, and political maneuvering. My hat goes off to Mr. Moore for his insights within this realm.

Moore delineates the decisions that executives make into two categories: important decisions and urgent decisions. Important decisions are decisions the executive considers *important* in the long run. Important decisions are typically about tomorrow, the future. That makes them less "edgy," or less critical, than urgent decisions, which require immediate attention. When you invest in your retirement account or put dollars into a college savings fund for your children, you are making *important* decisions. From a business perspective, the decision to develop a new product category is an important decision—one that won't pay off for quite some time but that is important to the long-term health of the enterprise.

Urgent decisions are any decisions that are made because immediate action is required. An urgent decision is critical—it must be taken care of immediately. Since every organization must survive today—or there will be no tomorrow—urgent decisions often take precedence over important decisions. For instance, if you risk default on a mortgage due to lack of funds, you may be forced to tap your retirement fund—very important dollars that you promised only to use in emergency situations. A C-Suite decision to reduce its workforce by 2 percent—and enact a hiring freeze—is an urgent decision meant to ensure that cost structure is immediately reduced.

A major challenge for many salespeople lies in simply understanding how organizations make money. This is essential, for in the world of customer moneymaking, ignorance is not bliss. In other words, it is nearly impossible to add value to something of which you are unaware. So, conducting conversations about how customers generate and sustain revenues is essential if one is to connect and add value to customer strategy.

Moneymaking conversations with executives are conducted on two fronts: today and tomorrow. You will need to discuss how revenues and profits are generated *today* and what changes need to be made to sustain profitable growth *tomorrow*. Whether you are calling on a Fortune 500 company, a midsize market leader, a small enterprise with 10 million in sales, or a one-woman band, this conversation is always relevant.

In the following pages, I've combined the ideas presented in *Blue Ocean Strategy* with Moore's ideas to explain how executives make decisions to perpetuate profitable growth.

THE MASTER STRATEGIC PLAN MATRIX

To understand how senior executives attempt to sustain growth requires classifying decisions into four quadrants. To help you visualize how the Blue and Red Oceans overlap with the important and urgent decisions, I've created the Master Strategic Plan Matrix shown in figure 5.1.

The matrix (to be read clockwise from the top left-hand quadrant) is divided into two rows (the two oceans) and two columns (the two types of decisions) that intersect to create four quadrants. The top row of the matrix is Blue Ocean decisions; the bottom row is Red Ocean decisions. The left column is for important decisions; the right column is for urgent decisions.

Based on these elements, the Master Strategic Plan Matrix shows how executives make the risk/reward decisions that sustain profitable growth. To help you gain a clear understanding of how to use and interpret the model, I will refer to the O.C. Tanner case study described earlier.

THE BIG FOUR DECISIONS

Categorizing organizational spend was a good first step in your quest to better understand client strategy. Now, you'll need to learn the big four decisions made by all senior executives in their quests to sustain the growth of their companies. The Master

FIGURE 5.1: THE MASTER STRATEGIC PLAN MATRIX

	Important Decisions	**Urgent Decisions**
Blue Ocean Strategies	I Innovation Decisions	II Implementation Decisions
Red Ocean Strategies	IV Outsourcing Decisions	III Optimization Decisions

Strategic Plan Matrix will help you understand and analyze these decisions. This is the big picture of corporate strategy—nothing overly complex or magical. Whether you're calling on a Fortune 500 enterprise, a mid-market leader, a small company with $10 million in revenues, a small consulting firm, or a local retailer, this model applies. Most important, grasping this fluid concept is the first step in understanding how to connect *your value proposition* to *their strategy*. When this happens, magic occurs!

Quadrant I: Innovation Decisions (Blue Ocean, Important)

Decisions in this quadrant revolve around the future; new markets, value, or offerings must be created for positive differentiation—the driver of Blue Ocean strategies. The real reward of innovation is premium profit margins. In this quadrant, competitive strategies are anticipated, core competencies evaluated, and future scenarios debated. For instance, leadership may be contemplating buying other companies that would enable a total solutions strategy. It is an important—but not urgent—decision since it has little impact on *today*. Organizations have become increasingly quarterly focused, and the "urgent-less" nature of this quadrant means that these decisions tend to be less of a priority in many organizations.

O.C. Tanner Case Study: Within this decision quadrant, the leadership team decided that a "total solutions" approach to recognition would radically separate the company from the crowd. A roll-up strategy was considered—buying other companies who could "fill out" the gaps in their solution sets. Although some minor acquisitions were made, leadership ultimately decided on a more organic growth strategy—rolling up their sleeves, building new capabilities, and figuring out how to best go to market with the new value proposition.

Quadrant II: Implementation Decisions (Blue Ocean, Urgent)

This is the domain of deploying the Blue Ocean strategies that have been created in QI. New products and services have been created. New markets have been targeted. In other words, investments have been made, and now its time to turn "potential" into "actual." The window is open, and the organization must implement quickly before competitors rush in. First mover advantage is often rewarded with market leadership, so the stakes are high. That makes *speed* critical in this quadrant—the organization must move quickly to capture new opportunities. Also in play are other prizes of successful Blue Ocean implementation—enhanced reputation, potential rebranding, or strategic repositioning.

O.C. Tanner Case Study: Now it was time to deploy the differentiated solutions upon which the leadership team had bet the future. Early in this phase, training the sales team how to have "business conversations" took center stage. Regional sales managers also met with salespeople to create action plans to stimulate activity with a greater number of senior level decision makers.

Quadrant III: Optimization Decisions (Red Ocean, Urgent)

In this quadrant, offerings and markets have now matured. Competition—the enemy of profit—has entered the fray, squeezing margins and slowing growth—problems Red Ocean strategies are designed to combat. In this stage, offerings are often subject to RFP and/or reverse-auction processes. Due to these factors, leaders turn their thoughts toward efficiency. Lowering costs and improving productivity is a key focus since raising customer prices is difficult in highly competitive markets. The primary focus of QIII is maintaining the legacy cash cow that still accounts for the largest majority of revenues—urgent dollars that pay the bills and enable the organization to survive for another day. The old saying "cash is king" captures the importance of QIII from a leadership perspective. Ensuring that more cash is coming into than going out of the organization never falls far from leadership attention. Nothing is more important than maintaining the day-to-day business—surviving today offers a chance to "get lucky" tomorrow. And in this new era of financial disruption and market turbulence, surviving is clearly no easy task—often requiring urgent decisions to ensure that the organization lives to see another day.

O.C. Tanner Case Study: In this province, the company needed to better protect the core business of the company—long-term service awards—from two entities: lowball-pricing "product" competitors and aggressive procurement departments eager to reduce everything to a price/product negotiation. One such strategy to improve productivity involved training salespeople to conduct annual strategy reviews with senior executives to illustrate the improved results the client was enjoying.

Part of this strategy also involved training salespeople how to better negotiate with procurement in a win-win manner. In other words, once senior customer executives were convinced of the connection of O.C. Tanner solutions to their strategy, negotiation with procurement might still be required. This would require O.C. Tanner salespeople to understand the motivation of procurement—to demonstrate to their own executives how they saved their companies money. From a negotiation perspective, this might require doing what Tom Muccio of P&G did with Wal-Mart—discovering hidden money that might be "saved," meaning hard or soft dollars that procurement personnel could show their own executives as a means to demonstrate their value.

In summary, Tanner's focus was on protecting the core offering by making it more strategic and integrating other Tanner solutions to help clients reach their goals.

Quadrant IV: Outsourcing Decisions (Red Ocean, Important)

In this final quadrant, leadership must answer the question, What should we not be doing? Valuable people and money need to be freed from the Red Ocean and redirected to the Blue Ocean for new differentiation strategies to succeed. Consequently, leadership may consider shedding certain business units that no longer fit with the new direction of the enterprise. Another example would be outsourcing, a strategy to consider when internal work could be done cheaper by external vendors. These are important decisions—as opposed to urgent—because outsourcing decisions typically impact the organization in the long run.

O.C. Tanner Case Study: The company needed to build a new technology platform if it was to succeed in its new "total solutions" strategy. But old legacy systems that needed constant updating were preventing the information systems department from helping in this area. Consequently, the company outsourced a portion of the coding of the new technology platform to speed to market this important Blue Ocean strategy.

EXERCISE

Remember, all the customer cares about is value. Based on that, which quadrants do your solutions most impact? See if you can identify why customers spend valuable capital and resources on your solutions. How does this spend ultimately tie into their core strategy? An important point to keep in mind is that QIII and QIV Red Ocean productivity solutions often free up critical customer resources that can be deployed for QII Blue Ocean initiatives.

Mickey Mouse Strategy?

Let's look at another company whose products and services you're likely to be familiar with to illustrate the master strategic plan of an organization.

Walt Disney Studios is the creator of all those wonderful movies you grew up with—*Snow White, Peter Pan, Pinocchio, The Little Mermaid, Aladdin,* and more. Today, computer generated movies like *Toy Story* and *Cars* have reinvented the animation category (Pixar is now owned by Disney). To help you recognize how easy it is to tie almost any company's strategies to the Master Strategic Plan Matrix, I've analyzed Disney's growth strategy based on articles and information the company has released (see figure 5.2).

QI: Innovation Decisions: I anticipate that a significant part of Disney's future revenue will be derived from online video on demand—movies delivered to consumers via the Web. Think of wireless technology beaming movies from the Internet to the family room television or to the minivan LCD screen. As you may be aware, more than a few global media and entertainment companies have been wounded by betting on this category (they were on the "bleeding edge"), but it appears to be a category ready to emerge from the doldrums.

QII: Implementation Decisions: QII decisions for Disney are still focused on DVD production and distribution. It is no secret that this is where movie studios have derived much of their revenue and profits over the last decade. A movie studio is often quite satisfied to break even on a film at the box office, simply recouping its production costs. The real money for movie studios is made on the back end in DVD sales. As for the future of DVDs, there are strong signs that this category has matured. For this reason, Disney Blu-ray DVD is emerging as its dominant QII strategy, including the rerelease of older films on that platform. This is important because Disney may have concerns that video-on-demand may be a bit slower to market than anticipated.

FIGURE 5.2: DISNEY'S MASTER STRATEGIC PLAN MATRIX

	Important Decisions	**Urgent Decisions**
Blue Ocean Strategies	I → Innovation Decisions Online Video	II Implementation Decisions DVD, Disney Blu-ray
Red Ocean Strategies	IV ← Outsourcing Decisions Dramatic movie productions (e.g., *The Royal Tenenbaums*)	III Optimization Decisions Family movie production (e.g., *The Incredibles*) and theatrical release

QIII: Optimization Decisions: Decisions in this quadrant are likely focused on digitally created animated films. Movies like *Monsters Inc.* and *Finding Nemo* represent Disney's stable of talent. Today, though, family entertainment has evolved into an intensely contested category. *Cinderella, Peter Pan,* and *Snow White* were never required to go head-to-head with the likes of *Shrek, Harry Potter,* and *The Simpsons* (or compete for dollars and attention with Nintendo's Wii). For Disney, release of family fare into national theaters is pure Red Ocean turf—slow growth and modest margins that reflect the new competitive realities of the entertainment industry.

QIV: Outsourcing Decisions: Outsourcing requires letting go. In this case, it means letting go of dramatic film production. Consider the critically acclaimed *The Royal Tenenbaums,* a movie released by Disney in 2001. Production was big in every way—big budget, big stars (Bill Murray, Ben Stiller, Gene Hackman)—and even bigger *losses* at the box office. For that reason, Disney was rumored to change its strategy for producing dramatic films, preferring to outsource dramatic film production to other studios as a means of reducing risk.

EXERCISE

Okay, you've got it! Now take a shot at applying the Master Strategic Plan Matrix to one of your customers by mapping out the strategy of a key customer.

THE ART OF THE POSSIBLE

The Master Strategic Plan Matrix represents how executives actually think about their businesses. They feel the need to make decisions in these four arenas on a regular basis, which means that they anticipate change in these areas. Unfortunately, many salespeople believe that the only reason a customer makes a change is to get cheaper prices, better quality, or faster turn-around. This is the distorted filter of product myopia. Our goal is to change this filter, breaking those heavy chains of habit that prevent salespeople from helping in the very areas where customers need it the most.

Timken, a $5.5 billion traditional bearing and steel company, is a well kept secret. Headquartered in Canton, Ohio, in the middle of a struggling rust-belt community, this well-managed company achieves profitable growth year after year. Tom Millis, senior vice president of global consulting solutions, has some interesting comments on the importance of his direct—and indirect—salespeople connecting to a bigger client picture:

> Being customer intimate is what it's all about. The importance of . . . understanding customer strategy cannot be overstated. The challenge is that a client cannot envision game-changing possibilities unless it is in the context of their strategic picture. In our world, we show customers how our "reliability solutions"—technology monitoring products and services—can make a radical impact on their productivity. To get customers to embrace this new way, though, requires that our salespeople are effective at linking these often-divergent offerings to their strategies—a feat easier said than done. After this initial connection is made, our salespeople need to be equally effective at creating and proffering solutions that leverage the diverse resources of our total organization, reaching high and wide to augment the customer vision.
>
> Articulate the art of the *possible*—that is what we must excel at. We are not as large or established as some of our competitors in this new field of reliability solutions, so we need to be smarter.

Any solution—whether a boring commoditized product or highly complex enterprise solution—is only relevant in the context of the strategies of the individual or organization. This is true whether a buyer has active or unrealized needs. Salespeople lose sight of this simple fact, often rushing ahead, showing their new-to-the-world product capabilities like excited kindergartners in show-and-tell.

But best-practices salespeople understand that real, thoughtful solutions can take wildly different forms. They understand that solution components are many and varied: training, services, expertise, alliances, products, support, symposiums, communications, platforms, and, dare we forget, products. Creating a customized solution that makes a real difference is not possible before first understanding the client's master strategy. Only then can one practice turning the impossible into the "art of the possible."

STICKY VALUE PROPOSITIONS

Remember the Velcro value principle described in chapter 3? This theory states that the more client strategies you can latch onto, the better. Put another way, the odds of your value proposition gaining acceptance is directly correlated to your ability to connect unique strains of value to the many stakeholders in a decision. To better understand this, let's continue following O.C. Tanner. Only this time, let's turn the tables and look at O.C. Tanner as a buyer of services.

The decision to hire a training—or consulting—firm can be a risky decision for executives for many reasons. For instance, a poor training experience with employees can lead to lost executive credibility that ultimately reverses momentum on an important new initiative.

Such was the case with our original discussions with O.C. Tanner. The company needed help, but investing in training to transition more than one hundred fifty salespeople was perceived as a risky endeavor. The company had invested in a popular sales training speaker the year before, and the event fell flat. To compound matters, the sales leadership had invested in a well-known strategic-selling sales training program a few years back that was not well received by the sales team. But with the stakes high for O.C. Tanner to transition its sales team, something needed to be done. This was a big decision for the leadership team. Not surprisingly, many executives had a voice in the decision, a norm in most complex solution sales.

Based on this scenario, in what ways did our value proposition "connect" to the needs of the major stakeholders in this important decision? Here's my perspective, broken down into the four quadrants of the Master Strategic Plan Matrix:

QI: Connecting to Innovation: The CEO, senior executive team, and board of directors had a huge stake in the new differentiation strategy created in Quadrant I. The company was betting its future—with much to gain or lose—based on the ability of the sales team to execute on this strategy. By suggesting and implementing training solutions that transitioned salespeople into businesspeople who sell, we were able to create key Quadrant I strategic value that enabled O.C. Tanner's future success.

QII: Connecting to Implementation: The executive vice president of sales had an obvious stake, but so did the EVP of marketing, whose team had created the new brand that would "grow legs" only if sales behavior changed. By training O.C. Tanner salespeople to attach their new brand—"Appreciation"—to the strategies of their customers, their new brand has achieved huge success.

QIII: Connecting to Optimization: Long-term service awards—the core product—was under attack from cheaper-priced competition. Revenue growth had stalled, and margins were slowly deteriorating. The chief financial officer, chief operations officer, and product managers were all acutely interested in a strategy that would protect the golden goose in a more-effective way. Once O.C. Tanner salespeople understood how to package core offerings within a strategic total solution, these same core products were less vulnerable to low-cost disruptive competitors. In addition, senior customer executives might actually step in when O.C. Tanner's core offerings were threatened, not wanting to disrupt the O.C. Tanner strategic value that enabled the accomplishment of a bigger strategic picture.

QIV: Connecting to Outsourcing: The chief technology officer needed to build a new technology platform for the total solutions strategy to be realized. This new platform might be developed in-house or outsourced. Yet, the key was for leadership to see some committed clients first as a way to reduce risk. The IT people were dependent on the sales team to gain these new clients. Since the Sogistics training taught salespeople how to sell divergent offerings that created major accounts, the risk of constructing the new technology platform—whether outsourced or otherwise—was eliminated.

In summary, for O.C. Tanner, the fact that our value proposition aligned so well with its strategy helped grease the decision skids. This was not without much internal debate and thoughtful consideration. When the decision to move ahead was made, many key people had a vested interest in the outcome—subsequently doing whatever they could to ensure that the sales force was supported in their efforts to transition. This led to a very successful project that drove radical sales productivity gains—especially around the ability to sell the new differentiation strategy upon which leadership had bet the future.

> **EXERCISE**
>
> Knowing what you now know, which customer quadrant(s) are you attempting to add value to? This is a critical question worthy of serious thought. On occasion, your answers may lead you to redefine what business you are actually in.

BLUE DEMAND, RED DEMAND

If you face the challenge of trying to create demand for your products—something every salesperson should ultimately be concerned about—the first sale you must make is selling a case for change within your customer organizations. If you can't convince them that change is in their best interest—that it furthers their strategic plans and positioning—you're dead in the water.

The best way to convince customers of the necessity of change is to demonstrate that your solution will have an impact on both their Blue and Red Ocean strategies. When your value proposition has an impact on both the differentiation *and* the productivity strategies of the customer, all stakeholders in the decision will be motivated to invest in you. The rule to follow is that the more quadrants of the Master Strategic Plan Matrix you have an impact on, the more value the customer will see. Since all the customer cares about is value, this will help you build a rock-solid case for change.

When this happens, it's like a grandmaster chess champion who anticipates three moves in advance. You just made a sale, although the deal may not be consummated for a few months. The customer may still be unaware of the Velcro connection at this point. But you aren't. You can feel confident that you've made the connections necessary to close the sale.

When considering which strategies to focus on as you attempt to build a case for change, keep this in mind: Any organization will take a great deal more risk if the risk furthers its Blue Ocean strategies—its vision, dreams, and ideas of a better future. This is especially important when selling divergent or complex offerings that buyers may be highly resistant to. To create demand for new (read risky) concepts, one must align with the Blue Ocean strategy of the client.

Conversely, expenditures focused solely on Red Ocean productivity improvement (QIII and QIV) often have difficulty gaining traction with executives. Why? Many senior executives do not see value in investing valuable resources in purely Red Ocean initiatives. This is already a slow-growth, margin-challenged area. And remember, overfeeding the Red Ocean at the expense of the Blue Ocean will eventually catch up, causing big problems in the long run.

But what if your value proposition is complex but not necessarily divergent and only affects the Red Ocean—that your offerings are solely about helping clients achieve more with less in their core business. If this is the case, don't fret. Instead, just expand your thinking a bit. A Red Ocean solution almost always frees up valuable resources—money and people that can be redirected to the Blue Ocean objectives of the company. Just don't expect the senior executives you're calling on to make this mental connection—they won't do your work for you. You'll need a mechanism called "General Recommendations" to clearly communicate how your solutions can affect both the Blue and Red Ocean strategies of the customer. I'll cover General Recommendations in the last few chapters of the book.

Understanding the master strategic plan of a customer isn't rocket science. All companies must innovate, deploy their innovations, optimize the cash cow, and, finally, let go of work that weighs the company down. Whether your customers are global organizations, midsize firms, or small, local entrepreneurs, they are all striving to get ahead, all fighting for survival.

In this manner, the Master Strategic Plan Matrix relates to individuals as well. Ever more frequently, individuals must reinvent because their core skills have become commodities in a competitive economy. In fact, that's what this book is about—the idea that salespeople need to personally reinvent themselves into something that customers find significantly more valuable.

Do you need to reinvent? If you're not sure, perhaps our next chapter can answer this question by helping you see that—in an ever-shrinking world—it's truly a whole new game.

CHAPTER SIX

CONNECTION MASTERY

The key to great customer conversations—real traction—lies in deep listening. But, it's hard to listen well when you're furiously scribbling notes, thinking of the next question, or trying to keep up with all the details of customer strategy. "Capture technology" is a huge advantage for sales teams interested in winning on a new know-how—business and strategic expertise.

—Mark Woodka, former senior director of emerging technologies, BEA

MEET GLENN MCCOY — COACH EXTRAORDINAIRE. Glenn is a baseball coach who specializes in teaching high school and college athletes how to improve their hitting performance. Now, there are many, many hitting coaches who offer personalized instruction, but few compare to Glenn. In fact, Glenn is legendary for his ability to take average athletes and turn them into extraordinary hitters.

Glenn's teams have won state titles. His daughter recently led her college fast-pitch softball team in hitting. And Glenn's squads are always the favorite to win league titles—the most feared by other teams. They follow a single mantra—win by out-slugging the competition. The statistics of his players speak volumes about Glenn's coaching ability—his trainees set new hitting records every year, raising the performance bar for each subsequent generation of players.

How does Glenn do it? Does he have some secret hitting formula? Hardly—Glenn teaches a standardized hitting methodology taught by many other coaches. Do his players outwork their competition, putting in long, grueling hours of hitting practice? Nope—Glenn thinks his players should work hard but stay balanced and enjoy other things in life outside of baseball. In fact, besides Glenn's passion for hitting, there is very little that separates him from other instructors—with one exception. Glenn calls it his "X factor" in creating great hitters.

What is Glenn's X factor? In a word, technology! And this technology, when combined with Glenn's instruction, doesn't just modestly improve hitters, it transforms them.

The first thing Glenn does with a new student class is demonstrate the important fundamentals of hitting—the key mechanics required to be an effective hitter. This usually generates more than a few yawns from those who have seen it all before.

Glenn's next step is to digitally videotape each student hitting against a pitching machine—nothing new there. Then, Glenn shows each hitter their video, asking each for a self-assessment of their hitting competence and swing mechanics. Most, he says, think they are pretty good hitters who require only minor tweaking of their skills.

Now, here's where the story gets interesting. Glenn then loads their videos into a software program he developed that contains film of professional players. Via split screen imagery on his laptop, he puts each student side-by-side with some of the greatest hitters ever to swing a bat—Manny Ramirez, Albert Pujols, Ken Griffey, and Olympian Cheryl Bustos.

Glenn says he never fails to get a reaction of amazement from even the most close-minded hitters as they observe their swings in perfect synchronization with those of professionals. This is when Glenn can truly begin coaching—breaking down individual swing mechanics and showing players where they generally excel and specifically falter. "There is nothing more humbling," Glenn says, "than the reality of seeing yourself compared to the very best." Remember my cello story? My daughter thought she was a pretty good cello player—until she heard the maestro. Great coaches understand that teaching a complex skill always begins by providing a *context for motivation.*

To illustrate this point, Glenn says he believes that individuals do not become "students of hitting" when they sign up for lessons, walk into his building for the first time, or step into the batting cage. Rather, most "arrive" when watching their swings compared to the very best hitters. That's when the switch is turned on.

Once the lessons have begun, battling complacency is the next battleground—good always being the enemy of great. When Glenn senses self-satisfaction creeping in, he moves his equipment outside to videotape students hitting in real game situations. This is a lesson of a different sort, since pitchers can do one thing machines cannot—think. Skilled pitchers change speed, location, and movement. As such, swings don't look as impressive—and both humility and openness to learning are restored. This sends an important message that *you're either humble or about to be humbled*—with the former mind-set a requisite for learning and growth.

Now that you understand the big picture of strategy—the subject of our last chapter—you'll soon need to learn the specific skills required to execute such nuanced conversations. But to accelerate assimilation, I need to teach you about one very important principle—*learning to learn.* In other words, to master a set of complex skills, it's important that you apply effective design to your learning. This will not only put you on the path to mastery, it will speed the journey as well.

In this chapter, I'm also going to teach you how to cheat—legally. In other words—and unlike many of your past teachers—I'm actually going to encourage you to cut learning corners. Everyone needs an edge, and yours is going to come in the form of creating and accessing cheat sheets that have one unusual characteristic—they talk. But before we discuss paper that talks, let's back up for a moment to our Glenn McCoy story.

PREPARE—CAPTURE—FEEDBACK: THE CYCLE OF MASTERY

Let's look at the method that has made Glenn McCoy so successful—a method of sound learning design for young hitters attempting to learn the complex skill of hitting a small ball thrown at high speeds.

First, Glenn asked students to prepare to hit—to think about what they needed to focus on when they were at bat. Next, Glenn captured them executing the skill via digital video and loaded that video into analytical software. Last, Glenn gave each hitter feedback, with a corresponding action plan that included suggested drills and a return date to the hitting cage to measure progress.

Prepare, capture, and *feedback*—this is the cycle required to gain mastery in any complex process, skill, or methodology.

But truth be told, the manner in which sales effectiveness training has been conducted has not structurally changed in decades. The process today usually goes like this: put people in a classroom, do some role-playing, and see what sticks. Unfortunately, once salespeople leave the training, there is little accountability to change. As a result, salespeople often gravitate back to the same old skills that they relied on in the past for success.

Mary Beth Walker, vice president of global business operations for Sun Microsystems, observed that

> Most salespeople rely on what they did yesterday to achieve success. Training presupposes that salespeople understand that they must think and act differently—for example, call on executives, discuss new forms of value, and stimulate demand. But, from my perspective, the challenge of change isn't in the classroom, it's in the field. It's very difficult to hold people accountable to what they learned in training when they conduct their real work with customers, which is often hidden from line managers. As a result, instead of improving, it's common for salespeople to revert back to what they find most comfortable—the old way of doing things.

From my perspective, sales training and books—even mine—are helpful learning mechanisms, but not game changers. In selling, real learning happens in the field, where feedback occurs. Unfortunately, customers don't often give you the detailed feedback you need to improve your skills. For instance, I'll bet you've never heard a customer say, "You didn't do a very good job of creating demand, asking me better questions, or connecting to my strategy." Instead, they politely say things like "Your price is too high," meaning that they really don't see the value of doing business with you.

The great Irish poet William Butler Yeats said, "Without action and accountability, dreams simply remain unfulfilled potential." So, let's you and I make a deal right now—a partnership. Your commitment is to view yourself as a "do-it-yourself" project, committing to whatever it takes to become a more valuable, strategic resource to your customers. My job is to provide you with two things: a best-practices selling framework (strategies, steps, and skills) and state-of-the-art technology that ensures your action and accountability.

Training + Technology + Accountability = Transformation of Productivity

The real lesson of Glenn McCoy's story is how the combination of training, technology, and accountability can radically improve productivity. I've described a basic training methodology that I'll delve into throughout the chapter. But I'm also going to introduce you to a game-changing technology that can help you constantly improve your mastery of this new sales approach.

This tool ensures that potential becomes reality in two important ways. First, it will help you be better prepared for critical sales calls. Second, it will help you get the critical feedback you need on an actual sales call—the adjustment mechanism required to master any complex skill. In truth, without feedback, there can rarely be meaningful change. It accomplishes this because it is a form of capture technology.

Capture technology is opening up a whole new world for salespeople. To get a sense of its potential, see if you can imagine the following:

Imagine perfect preparation: All salespeople love cheat sheets. Imagine being able to quickly create *custom* cheat sheets—that talk. Capture technology allows you to link audio recordings (from a sales training seminar, a new product overview, or a CEO's speech about his company's strategies, for example) to specific parts of a document. This capability allows your documents to contain thousands of verbal nuggets of information. As you tap on the hard-copy cheat sheet before or during a call, complex product sheets come alive, stories from other subject matter experts are told, and details about the strategies of the company you're about to call on are explained. In other words, you get the right information at the right time—ensuring an effective call that adds value to the customer. Talking cheat sheets will not only improve your ability to become a better salesperson, they will also drastically improve the quality of your relationships with the executives on whom you call.

Imagine a perfect capture: Salespeople are in the relationship business, and customer conversations are the building blocks to a quality relationship. The reality for consultative salespeople is that customers talk about twenty times faster than our ability to take notes. Research shows that this leads to the loss of valuable information. Furthermore, organizations are often complex organisms, and information can easily fly overhead in a flurry of exchange. Capture technology allows you to capture and archive customer conversations *with their full approval*— ensuring that valuable strategic nuggets are fully captured 100 percent of the time. And audio recordings of a conversation are always perfectly synchronized to the notes you take, requiring you to simply tap the specific note to rehear the conversation at that point in time.

Imagine perfect feedback: As I've said, it's the sales calls made early in the cycle that determine sales success or failure. How often do you get feedback from your manager on your early sales calls—coaching that constructively examines how you handled each aspect of the call? If you're like most salespeople, probably not much. With capture technology, your manager can listen to the recording of an entire call with you and give you clear, specific feedback on what seemed to work and what didn't. And possibly even more important, you can listen to your own calls—particularly when you're working within a proven selling framework—and hear where you won or lost a customer. And that information is available 24/7—at your convenience, not your manager's—to help you perpetually improve the quality of your sales calls.

Coolest Invention Ever for Sales Effectiveness

As salespeople, we take many technologies for granted today—email, laptops, and cellular telephony. These technologies began as dreams, and today they have changed the world.

That said, I am not a technology guy. I have no interest in being the first in my group to have the latest gadget. I like to keep things simple, and too often technology complicates simple matters. However, I positively love technology that gives me a competitive edge, makes my job easier, and adds value to my customers.

My company has recently adopted a new technology for salespeople and sales teams that enables them to better prepare for calls, capture customer conversations, and gain feedback on field performance. What's distinctive about this technology is that it doesn't require a laptop, a connection to the Internet, or a BlackBerry to do its job. And, rather than just adding internal value to the organization, this one also offers external value to the customers you call on. Best of all, it requires merely a pen and a notepad—the two standard tools all salespeople currently use, whether in the field or in the office.

This new tool is called a Sogistics Smartpen—a fully functioning 1.3-ounce writing instrument with computing power built in. It looks and feels like a pen, but it's actually a computer in disguise. Livescribe offers the Pulse smartpen, and we have our own version called the Sogistics Smartpen. The difference between the two is the total system and proprietary software we've built into and around our Smartpen—a sales productivity improvement system that allows salespeople to learn our selling methodology, access Sogistics cheat sheets, create their own custom cheat sheets, and capture sales conversations in a way that allows constructive feedback.

Here's how it works. The Sogistics Smartpen records audio as you take critical customer notes—or summarize your notes verbally after important customer conversations. As you converse with customers, the Sogistics Smartpen magically connects the recorded audio to what you are writing at that time—on a standard notepad, not a special note-taking laptop. All you need to do is go back to any page in your notes and tap the pen on a word. The pen immediately begins "talking" to you—playing the exact audio that was recorded at the precise moment you wrote your notes.

When you first use the Sogistics Smartpen, it seems like absolute magic. But this is no toy or trick. Rather, it is a serious business tool that radically improves customer conversations. A conversation that revolves around an opportunity can be extremely difficult to absorb and document at the same time. For example, it is essential that you pay attention to what is being communicated, listening in-depth to strategies and issues and creating fluent dialogue that builds on customer responses. That means you need to pay more attention to what is being said and less on furiously taking notes.

The irony of note taking is that it both helps and hinders good communication. Few can recall all the important specifics of a conversation, so penning key comments is essential. But your customers and prospects talk a lot faster than you can capture notes, so you end up losing a lot of valuable insight in a furious note-taking scramble. In this way, comprehension is hindered. Trying to keep up is one thing, and understanding your notes later on is quite another. I don't know about you, but I often have difficulty reading my own notes after a sales call, or recalling exactly what was said at the moment I was capturing a note. This makes it extremely difficult to put together subsequent presentations, proposals, or documents that correctly incorporate the voice of the customer.

These communication constraints are now a thing of the past. With this unique mechanism that looks and feels like a normal pen, you can literally go back to client notes from many months earlier, tapping a word on the page to hear that exact moment in time replayed.

The concept of a pen that captures information digitally has been around for over a decade—LeapFrog being one of the first serious entrants. And today, the capture of audio via a pen device is possible in a number of ways.

LEGAL CHEATING: PREPARING FOR THE CALL

Salespeople who want to transform need transformative tools. And cheat sheets are a key transformative tool for great preparation. Many salespeople call on diverse industries and functional departments. As a result, they end up being jacks-of-all-trades, masters of none. This generalist reality gets in the way of having meaningful conversations that gain traction with executives. Cheat sheets solve this problem by allowing you to more quickly prepare for complex opportunities by highlighting critical information that you feel is essential to grasp for an upcoming call. Cheat sheets ultimately enable you to better prepare for critical sales calls—no easy task when calling on executives who run complex organizations.

Cheat sheet categories can be many and varied. All vastly improve sales call preparation.

- *Sales effectiveness cheat sheets:* Following a sales framework like the one written about in this book can be a difficult task early on. Sales effectiveness cheat sheets serve as a road map to the appropriate strategies, skills, and steps that must be followed to ensure quality sales calls. For instance, you might need some quick help creating call strategy, preparing a sophisticated questioning document, or engaging in an important negotiation. A good cheat sheet enables

Graphic by Bill Hinsch, Learning Visuals.com

An example of a commercially available 'Talking Cheat Sheet'© - this one a verbal field guide
that explains the key concepts and strategies from this book (www.sogisticssmartpen.com)
(illustration by graphic designer/artist Lindsey Frymyer).

you to quickly review important tips and tactics at the ideal moment.

- *Technical cheat sheets:* Today, new products, services, and capabilities are being released at breakneck speeds. For salespeople, trying to keep up seems next to impossible. In fact, training sales teams on new product releases and complex technologies has made national sales meetings look more like college exam week—on steroids! With technical cheat sheets, you can highlight specifications, data, benefits, and costs to give you an edge during calls.

- *Industry cheat sheets:* Many salespeople sell across industry boundaries. An average week might see the same salesperson make calls to the pharmaceutical, software, hospitality, and manufacturing industries. Each industry has its own uniqueness, trends, and language. Cheat sheets help you quickly ramp-up on industry knowledge and nomenclature—just in time, not a moment before you need it.

- *Functional title/department cheat sheets:* Salespeople need to be increasingly expansive in the departments they call on. Selling total solutions and integrated value to an enterprise demands different discussions with different people around different ways of doing jobs. This strategy requires salespeople to meet with different functional departments: marketing, finance, operations, quality assurance, and information technology. This puts many salespeople outside their comfort zone since each of these disciplines has its own nomenclature, discipline, trends, and uniqueness. Department cheat sheets give salespeople a leg up in their ability to have more intelligent conversations when encountering new functional areas.

- *Customer cheat sheets:* Company cheat sheets are where client vision, strategy, objectives, constraints, culture, products/services, and relationships can be documented—in a condensed *one-page* sheet. Creating a one-page sheet allows salespeople to jog memories before encountering clients and prospects, doing a quick review before engaging in important dialogue.
- *Internal best practices cheat sheets:* You probably have some excellent salespeople and account managers in your company who do things in a best practices manner. The challenge lies in getting information out of their heads and into the practices of your other salespeople. Cheat sheets are the perfect way to capture how the very best do their work—in a manner that can be re-tapped time and again by those with less experience.

Either you—or the people you work with—will create many of these cheat sheets. It's simple and easy to do, and it will become a mechanism you revisit again and again for the important Cliffs-Notes of any situation. The key is to keep the sheets simple. However, you also need to make sure that you are highlighting the information that is most critical. This is one place where the Sogistics Smartpen technology described in the case study can be effective.

If you use the Sogistics Smartpen to create your cheat sheets, you'll gain a new perspective of the saying "A picture is worth a thousand words." In the case of capture technology, a picture is no longer just a simple illustration or photograph. It actually comes alive, being transformed into hundreds of pieces of important information previously hidden from sight.

ELEPHANT MEMORY: CAPTURING THE CALL

It is my recommendation that you record important sales calls using capture technology. But, the technology needs to be unobtrusive so as not to inhibit open dialogue with the customer you're calling on. You may be wondering, are customers really open to having conversations captured in this manner? Surprisingly, yes. Salespeople have always captured customer information via notes—this is just an expanded version of this process. And, when positioned properly, customers appreciate the fact that you want to capture the more complex nuances of their business (in fact, many will encourage you to do so). Clients also value that other experts in your company will be confidentially clued in to their situation—this nets them better ideas, solutions, and results. You need to ask for their permission, of course, but rest assured that most clients are open to capture technology for one simple reason—its adds value to their strategy.

Not all customers want conversations captured, and there are obvious scenarios of propriety where salespeople would not ask permission for capture. In these cases, the customer conversation is captured via a summary document that is composed immediately after the call. This forces salespeople to condense information when it is fresh in their mind, expanding on key points verbally versus wasting time keyboarding. Remember, since customers can talk twenty times faster than you can take notes, this call summary capability can serve as a more thorough, cogent, and time-saving vehicle for already time-constrained salespeople.

What users of capture technology have discovered is that reviewing critical customer conversations after the fact is extremely worthwhile. Valuable information is uncovered by simply listening to key parts of a past conversation. This means that lost information is recaptured. And this is critical for those salespeople who need to advance to proposals or recommendations (a key step we'll discuss in chapter 10). Today, information equals money, so capturing all important nuggets of information is essential in order to optimize an opportunity.

Many complex sales calls require joint calls. If you'll be bringing others to the client table—subject matter experts, executives, and product managers—you'll find this capture capability the perfect ramp-up mechanism. Others need simply listen to the actual customer conversation. They'll feel like they were at the first meeting, and consequently they'll be much better prepared to add value to the client situation in future interactions.

Again, the Sogistics Smartpen offers some distinct benefits in this area. For example, instead of having to fast-forward or rewind through a sixty-minute conversation hunting for a single piece of information, you can tap the part of your notes where that information was discussed and immediately hear that part of the conversation. And as for inputting data into your CRM database after the call—something all salespeople disdain—consider it a thing of the past. This technology converts summarized handwritten notes into readable text that can be imported into your CRM software. All you need do is cradle your Sogistics Smartpen and your notes are immediately uploaded to your computer; from there, it's a quick step to your CRM database.

STRATEGIC COACH: CALL FEEDBACK

Glenn McCoy understands that feedback is the key to change. Without a mechanism that captures live performance and explicitly compares that performance to those who are at the top of their game, real change will not happen. In a similar vein, when salespeople hear their actual calls in comparison to a standardized, best-practices sales methodology, the experience can be eye-opening *and* mind opening.

Again, feedback is critical to mastery of a complex discipline or skill. Without feedback, only marginal progress will occur. Once a call is captured, you must actually do something with that recording to ensure that this final step of mastery is accomplished. If you capture critical calls but never listen to them, what's the point? If you capture your calls and your manager never listens to them, what have you gained? In other words, the adage that "hindsight is 20/20" is true. So make sure you're either self-coaching or using a third-party coach to ensure that you're both maximizing your potential and optimizing each of your valuable selling opportunities.

For savvy sales leaders and managers, this feedback capability is indeed the Holy Grail of sales force effectiveness. Since selective customer conversations conducted in the field can now be immediately assessed with capture technology, the opportunity for quickly coaching salespeople to higher performance is finally possible. This moves training from the classroom to the field— the place of execution where real accountability and change occur. Glenn McCoy would be proud.

Can salespeople act as their own coaches? In certain situations, of course. But a salesperson who *always* serves as his own coach is like the lawyer who represents himself—both have a fool for a client.

AN UNMANAGEABLE PROFESSION NO MORE

This chapter was born because of my increasing frustration with the training/execution gap in the sales profession. Unlike other disciplines, a sale is made in the minds and offices of a customer.

This is where our particular knowledge work occurs. As such, this is where it must be managed. Most would agree that this reality has made sales a largely unmanageable profession, often unaccountable to change.

But the mastery process of preparation, capture, feedback—particularly when combined with the capture technology described in this chapter—fills in pieces long missing in the sales effectiveness puzzle. The mastery process is simple—no thirty-two steps here. And capture technology is simple to use and cost-effective. The Sogistics Smartpen—particularly when part of a total sales productivity process—adds immediate and practical value to all three of the critical elements required for mastery—preparation, capture, and feedback. This divergent technology radically improves how each of these jobs is accomplished.

Remember, though, technology is just a tool and just one component of the mastery equation. The real change comes in the skills and competencies you employ during your calls. In other words, you'll need to learn some new skills—and unique sales steps—if your ultimate goal is to gain a seat at the table. And our next chapter talks about the most important skill of all in having truly meaningful executive conversations—FOCAS!

CHAPTER SEVEN
CONVERSATIONS THAT CONNECT

I always tell my salespeople that *no one cares about your new technology*. Talk about *business*—not software. The irony is that the less our salespeople talk about our products, the more products they sell.

—David Peckinpaugh, former executive vice president of sales and
   marketing, Experient

DO YOU LIKE PEANUT BUTTER and jelly sandwiches? When I was growing up, my mother would pack me a peanut butter and jelly sandwich every day for lunch. At school, I'd take it out of the brown bag, unwrap it from the wax paper, and have lunch with my friends. The jelly flavor didn't matter much—grape, strawberry, or peach. Truth be told, I was a PB and J fanatic!

Now, some of my buddies were biased toward jelly sandwiches—all sizzle. Others liked their sandwiches with peanut butter only—substance, but no sizzle. My perspective was that both groups had defective taste buds. Peanut butter without the jelly—or vice versa—just didn't cut it. For me, it was the *combination* of the two that made for such a great taste.

And so it goes for a meaningful conversation with a senior executive. Making a connection will require the combination of two important ingredients:

1. **A strategic blueprint:** This will tell you how organizations sustain profitable growth.
2. **A questioning structure:** This will enable you to quickly connect to executive strategy.

You already know the first ingredient—the Master Strategic Plan Matrix of how organizations sustain profitable growth. This one is critical since it is the "business filter" hardwired into all senior executive brains—either at birth (for some) or in business school (for most). Any discussion in which you attempt to connect to their strategy will be passing through this filter, so you'll need to bring this blueprint to the table every time.

Yet if this single mental schema is all that's in your brown bag, you'll be missing one very important ingredient—and what you'll unwrap won't taste very good to you or your new executive friend. Consequently, you'll never be invited back to show valuable ideas and options—the next step in the sales process. In fact, this first meeting is so crucial when you're trying to connect with executives, I've devoted three chapters to it.

So, if your goal is for both parties to leave the very first encounter sated and looking forward to another one, you'll want to pay particularly close attention to this discussion of the "questioning ingredient" needed to tastefully connect with executives. Now, you won't need to learn how to do this if the executives you call on have defective taste buds, but don't count on it. I'll bet their moms packed them peanut butter and jelly sandwiches when they were kids, too, so it's best to come prepared.

Let's start by looking at how the executive psyche is different from the mid-level manager psyche, a key element in understanding the approach you need to take with higher-level contacts.

EXECUTIVE VELCRO

One of the biggest challenges salespeople face is fighting for scarce customer dollars. This is why all salespeople *need* to call at the executive level: executives dictate strategy; strategy dictates spend. And the fact that senior executives can make discretionary spend decisions "unconstrained by normal budgets" make them a very popular audience with salespeople. If an executive likes your solutions, the "no money" objection is negated. They will find the money to fund your solutions. This is a polite way of saying that senior executives can steal budget dollars from lower-ranking managers if they think *you* have a better way to accomplish *their* strategies. Of course, this is why senior executives are more important to salespeople than are the lower-ranking managers.

So how do you get an executive to redirect scarce dollars toward your solutions? Like any situation where complexity is involved, overcoming this challenge will require an effective call strategy. And good strategy always covers two important elements: what to do and what *not* to do. Selling to senior executives is an entirely different game from selling at mid-levels. The research and case studies in this book prove that the sales competencies that work with mid-level personnel actually *get in the way* of success when calling higher up the ladder. Showing up for an appointment at the senior level and executing the wrong strategy—a strategy designed for mid-level managers—is akin to a train wreck for your reputation. And your reputation—and the reputation of the company you represent—is the most important asset of any customer-intimate seller.

Focus on the Strategic, Not the Tactical

What must *not* happen when attempting to create demand with senior executives is a discussion that turns to the tactical—your products and services. As we've already discussed, product and service value is the language of mid-level managers, not executives. For less-experienced salespeople, this "no products discussed" rule can be maddeningly difficult to follow because it seems so counterintuitive. After all, how can one sell products if one doesn't talk about products? We will discuss this later in appropriate detail, but rest assured that if your conversation with a senior executive turns to features and benefits, the opportunity will die—sooner rather than later. Some prefer this quicker death to watching an opportunity experience a slow dissipation over many months and eventually reaching "no decision"—but this is like debating whether losing by forty points is better than losing by a field goal. At the end of the day, losing is losing, and the customer doesn't award prizes for effort or second place finishes.

Focus on Building a Foundation, Not Pushing a Product

Product push techniques, like doing presentations on your first call to a senior executive, can be a deceptive apparition—one that appears to work early on, but in fact is laying the groundwork for failure. The deception occurs because senior executive prospects often welcome presentations about new technologies and game-changing value propositions. Unfortunately, the enthusiasm predictably fizzles after months of follow-up meetings. "We'll look at it again next budget season," is the likely deathblow to a large opportunity that failed to be properly bridged from curiosity to commitment.

When a postmortem is conducted on the deceased opportunity, rarely is the initial presentation seen as the cause of death. Yet, this is where the blame most often lies. The problem is that the time lapse between the dog and pony show and the final no is so distant that there seems no possible correlation to failure. And didn't the presentation do its initial job of advancing the selling cycle? Predictably, the coroner rules the death accidental. "It was no one's fault," sales executives declare, "and nothing could have been done to prevent this outcome." Tragically, this lack of learning prevents the same events from being repeated in the future.

In reality, these common postmortems fail to recognize what was NOT done early in the selling cycle—construction of a business case for change tied directly to the core strategies of the prospect. As sure as night follows day, a large resource spend—especially one fraught with the risk associated with a divergent offering—will be put under the microscope in the weeks and months that follow an initial presentation. Predictably, the opportunity tumbles like a house of cards.

Businesspeople who sell understand this predictable dynamic, and as a result they ignore the Sirens' lure of the product pitch early on. They understand that until a change foundation is built, even the most tantalizing presentation will rarely withstand the heavy scrutiny sure to follow by others with a voice in the decision. Consequently, their preference is to quickly engage executives in discussions about matters that seem totally unrelated to the offerings themselves—substantive things like the customer's differentiation strategies, productivity objectives, competitive landscape, and critical roadblocks. This critical information is impossible to learn, of course, if the salesperson chooses to talk and present—do the "razzle dazzle" as they say—instead of listen and converse in the context of customer strategy. For those attempting to create demand for their solutions, data assuredly demonstrates that executive presentations on divergent—or high-risk—solutions too early in the sales process are a sure recipe for disaster (no matter how elaborate or convincing the multimedia). At a minimum, it ends up in a quick "thanks, but no thanks." At worst, the presentation path ends up consuming vast sales resources, chasing elusive rabbits down very expensive rabbit holes.

Focus on Future Opportunity, Not Today's Pain

Another challenge faced by salespeople in their quest to redirect customer spend toward their solutions lies in understanding that the sales competencies that work with mid-level managers do not translate to calls on senior executives. A quintessential sales technique that is effective with mid-level personnel but rarely effective with executives is the classic "pain based" questioning model taught as gospel in sales-training classrooms for over a quarter century. Most salespeople believe they need to find and remove buyer pain on sales calls. This strategy is hard to disagree with, assuming one is making calls to supervisors, mid-level managers, and even procurement personnel. But as a senior executive call strategy, it leads sellers down the wrong path.

Let's look at how a popular pain or problem question can derail a conversation with a senior executive: "What's keeping you up at night?" This question will resonate with mid-level people whose primary job is to avoid mistakes. This is because mid-level personnel are essentially tasked with executing the strategy of others, and an error in execution means possible criticism from the boss (something to be avoided at all costs). That's why sales questions that explore problems like poor quality or slow turnaround often resonate with mid-level people.

But higher-level executives think differently, and they do not make decisions based on the avoidance of criticism from higher authority. Their attention is *not* on the tactical problems of the day—these are the responsibility of lower-ranking managers. Instead, senior executives concern themselves with what new forms of value the company might deliver to customers, which new customers it should engage, and where it should best spend valuable resources. Their thinking is *future focused*. Although senior people spend 80 percent of their time on *today* issues, it's the 20 percent of time spent on *future-focused thinking* that weights most heavily in importance.

As such, much of executive time is spent thinking, meeting, and talking about *opportunities*. Opportunities require a forward-thinking mind-set. Executive contemplation in this realm often revolves around new alliances, new markets, new technologies, and new innovation that might help distance their companies from the competition. They ponder, "Is there an opportunity to be a disrupter in our markets?" The key word in this reflection is *opportunity*.

Consequently, questions that examine the "not happened yet" would be far more likely to elicit a thought-provoking conversation that appeals to the opportunistic psyche of an executive.

Can you see the disaster coming? For salespeople riding on the pain train, questions like "What's keeping you up at night?" completely derail the conversation. (Note to all salespeople: senior executives *are not* looking for a cure to insomnia.) Senior executives are a very future-focused group of people, and for good reason. Topics of sustainability, innovation, and competitive separation have moved to the senior executives' front burners. Why? The new realities discussed in chapter 3 are commoditizing offerings at a blinding pace. That's why discussions focused on differentiation and productivity—rather than today's pain—are far more likely to resonate at executive levels.

That's not to imply that executives don't think a lot about hitting the quarterly numbers—they do, and spend a great deal of time here. But a conversation that ignores the strategic (future opportunities) at the expense of the tactical (present pain) is half-baked at best, like peanut butter without the jelly.

Should you venture down this wrong track, you will be politely—but quickly—escorted downstairs and introduced to those people responsible for buying tactical products and services, who have little power to make discretionary spend decisions.

How to Identify a Powerful Decision Maker

Elliot Jacques was a Canadian-born psychologist who spent decades researching organizational hierarchies. One of his landmark studies examined how one can determine the degree of power an individual has in an organization. Before reading ahead, what do you think the answer is? I often ask this question of sales teams, and the answer never ceases to generate a collective aha!

What Jacques's research found was that true decision-making power did not necessarily correlate to title. Nor did individual power relate to how large a budget—or amount of discretionary spend—a person controlled. If you guessed that the key factor was the number of employees that reported to the individual, guess again. These were all secondary—not primary—factors that determined how much personal power an individual possessed within an organization.

What Jacques's research proved is that individual power is best determined by one variable above all else—the time horizon an individual makes a decision in. Simply, the people at the lowest levels of organizations deal in the shortest time horizons, which frequently means "right now" or "today." In other words, people at the lowest levels of an organization rarely make decisions that affect the future. As one moves up the organizational ladder, what increases is the amount of "future decision authority" one has. Many times, though, the people with the real power in an organization do not possess the biggest titles. If you look at an organizational chart, very powerful people may actually have less-powerful people above them. Their future decision-making authority clearly exceeds that of their bosses. These are the people who others in the organization go to when they need a decision that directly affects their abilities to get a job done.

By categorizing people according to decision time horizon, an organizational hierarchy could correctly be deduced, thus determining who *really* has power and influence in decisions.

In summary, the people with the most power were the ones who always dealt in the longest decision time horizons. They weren't necessarily the people with the biggest titles, spend, or direct reports. But, 100 percent of the time—in study after study—the people with the most decision-making power in an enterprise dealt in the longest time horizons.

THE CRITICAL FIRST STEP

Most salespeople are familiar with the process of discovery— that initial critical conversation with at least one key person in the decision base. In the best cases, that person is a senior executive. You may use different names for this critical first step, but it's something all salespeople have to execute.

How a seller approaches and executes the discovery process will determine the ultimate outcome of the sale: a quick lose, a slow decline to no decision, or a win. If this first step is executed well, the chances for closing the deal—even in very long selling cycles—skyrocket. The purpose of your call is not to see *how* you can help, but *if* you can add value to their strategy. To do that will require you to learn a bit more about how they go about things, information that goes beyond the Web research you did before this call.

Researching clients before a call is imperative, something that really doesn't need to be said. Learning about the customer organization by visiting their website, doing Internet research, examining annual reports, etc., is something that all serious sales professionals do. And this is where you find your preliminary information to assess using the Master Strategic Plan Matrix. But, it is important to note that the type of information you'll learn by executing FOCAS is not data that are likely to be published on a website. For instance, although a K-10 or annual report might reference some key strategies, it rarely fills in the true strategic picture of an organization. Companies rarely publish information about their real strategies, understanding that such exposure makes them vulnerable to plotting competition.

The best analogy I can offer is the difference between reading a magazine article about a CEO versus having an intimate discussion with that same person. Whatever your experience, the insight you captured from the conversation will undoubtedly give you an entirely different—and infinitely more accurate—portrayal of that individual from a real-world perspective.

Gaining an in-depth understanding of the customer does not happen on just one call. Discovery is where the process begins. As such, this makes discovery the most important sales call of all. Learn how to execute a discovery call effectively, and you've learned the platinum competence that you'll use time and again. But, like any complex skill, the devil is in the details.

Following are the four parts of a discovery:

1. **Approach:** A one- to two-minute high-level overview that gives the prospect some important background information on your company.

2. **Questioning:** A twenty-minute to two-hour discussion to learn as much relevant information about the prospect as possible.
3. **Summary:** A quick "Here's what I heard . . ." recap.
4. **Progression:** A recommendation for next steps.

In the approach, you will cover two important pieces of information: what you do and the purpose of your call. "What you do" is your strategic positioning statement—something you probably grapple with. This is the statement spoken in simple language that helps the customer understand what you do best. The important point here is to not describe your company as a "product" company, a very easy and common mistake. Remember, you are in the *results* business—high-impact results—and if you don't communicate this quickly to a senior executive you immediately risk misalignment and loss of interest.

The next step—and the most important part of the discovery—is the questioning process, the ingredient that, combined with a strategic blueprint, will be your key to building executive connections. If you can't do this well, you'll never be able to have connecting conversations with executives. To help you, I will teach you how to FOCAS.

I believe that training a sales force to excel in important subtleties makes all the difference in terms of winning or losing: delivering an approach that clearly articulates your passion and purpose—versus a mundane description where buyers politely nod—but fails to grab real attention; attempting to learn elements of customer strategy—before walking in the door; and preparing thoughtful questions that arouse curiosity—instead of lobbing pedestrian "open-ended" questions that lead to un-sticky conversations.

—Bill Horrigan, director of sales, Tribute Software

FOCAS!

This chapter will introduce you to a questioning structure to guide your initial meetings with executives. I call it *FOCAS*. When you learn how to execute FOCAS, you'll have gained the master competency required to gain traction with senior executives.

FOCAS is a critical piece of your connect-to-strategy puzzle—and ideally suited to complement the Master Strategic Plan Matrix you learned in chapter 5 (see figure 7.1). This method will help you arouse curiosity, broaden options, stimulate demand, transcend brands, promote concepts, resonate quickly, and connect intellectually during your conversations with senior executives.

Regardless of how salespeople describe it, this is what best-practices sellers *do* in interactions with prospects and customers. Some execute this competency "unconsciously"; others are consciously competent. Regardless, this questioning process represents best practices in the sales profession. The people who use this technique are able to stimulate demand, an especially important skill when selling divergent offerings.

FOCAS is an acronym with each letter signifying a type of question. Each type of question is unique in its intent and function. Broken into its components, the FOCAS questioning model is as follows:

- Fact Questions
- Objective Questions
- Concern Questions
- Anchor Questions
- Solution Questions

Understanding these five types of FOCAS questions is so critical that I will spend the next two chapters delving into each

FIGURE 7.1: THE FOCAS APPROACH TO SELLING STRATEGIC VA

	Important Decisions	Urgent Deci......
Blue Ocean Strategies	I Innovation Decisions	II Implementation Decisions
	FOCAS Fact questions Objective questions Concern questions Anchor questions Solution questions	
Red Ocean Strategies	IV Outsourcing Decisions	III Optimization Decisions

category, explaining how to use the model to connect with executives right from the start. Before I do, however, I need to explain why FOCAS is so effective and how best to implement it.

The FOCAS model allows you to transcend negative pain-based questioning, helping you learn what an organization is *attempting to create*. This dialogue is much more positive in tone, and it will generate valuable information to help you build your case for change.

Getting Past the Hot Stove

Becoming strategically valuable requires you to engage those senior level executives who make the big-bet decisions for their organizations. For some salespeople—and perhaps you—this may be viewed as a very uncomfortable task. Why? Mark

Twain's aphorism "A cat that jumps on a hot stove will never jump on a stove again—even if the stove is cold" explains it well. Product-driven salespeople who lack the skills to call on senior executives are reticent to return to a place where they've been burned in the past. When one gets curtly dismissed by senior executives for engaging in tactical, product-value discussions, bad memories can scar sales initiative forever.

This is one of the benefits of FOCAS. The simple, adaptable questioning model will give you the tools and confidence to overcome your hot stove issues and communicate effectively with executives.

THE FOURTH DIMENSION

The FOCAS questioning model was built to be flexible in four important ways. This four-dimensional flexibility is critical: You probably regularly find yourself in varied and challenging sales call scenarios, so cookie-cutter just won't due. What is required is a structure that you can adjust to fit the unique scenarios you face. Four-dimensional flexibility breaks down into the following areas:

1. **Title flexibility:** Organizations are an alphabet soup of titles, with levels ranging from C (CEO, COO) to D (director) to V (vice president) to M (manager) to S (supervisory). My assumption is that you may land in front of many different types of people who have varying degrees of power and influence in decision making. More often than not, you land at mid-management levels (S, M, and V), not the C-suite (or even D-suite). But in the words of my father, beggars cannot often afford to be choosers. In these mid-

level manager encounters, your questioning structure must *enable introductions up the food chain*. In other words, your discussions with the budget constrained must motivate these managers to introduce you to more senior people in their organizations. FOCAS enables this upward-mobility introduction strategy.

2. **Time flexibility:** FOCAS is also a very time flexible mechanism, allowing you to expand or collapse to the meeting time, whether it's twenty minutes or two hours. When time is short, FOCAS can help you cut through the clutter to get to the "naked" essence of a situation.

3. **Strategic flexibility:** Remaining strategically flexible will allow you to stretch from the macro to the micro strategies of the client. You will be able to deploy FOCAS according to the strategic range of the person you are dealing with. In other words, you could ask FOCAS questions to learn the big picture strategy of an organization—the mountaintop view—in one meeting, and you could direct FOCAS questions exclusively to a specific strategic quadrant in another meeting. For example, if your solutions primarily have an impact on QIII (Red Ocean, optimization, accomplish more with less), then you could deploy FOCAS in this direction.

   For situations in which executives cannot strategically see the broader implications of your solutions, FOCAS will help you peel the onion, guiding executives to realize the systemic value. This last point is especially critical for those selling concepts that impact the entire enterprise.

4. **Motivation flexibility:** Last, FOCAS helps you cover both sides of the buyer motivation to change—problems *and* opportunities. Executives and managers are a widely varied lot. Although senior executives are typically more opportunistic in nature than lower-ranking managers, sometimes

this psychology works in reverse. In other words, the mid-level manager you're dealing with is the forward-thinking opportunist, while the senior executive in the very same company is driven to avoid problems and criticism. FOCAS gives you the flexibility to determine this very important "psychology to change" dimension and adjust your questioning approach accordingly.

I've spent the majority of this chapter discussing the "why" of FOCAS. Understanding why a new tool is important is a critical first step. Now let's move on to our next chapter, which will cover the "what and how"—*what* FOCAS stands for, and *how* you can quickly learn this important skill.

Ready for a new FOCAS?

CHAPTER EIGHT

FOCAS ON CUSTOMER STRATEGY

What makes FOCAS so effective is that it keeps conversations centered on where value can be potentially added—often opportunities, not problem-removal. This makes it very customer friendly. I can think of no better competence for salespeople to learn. It puts an exclamation point on the purpose of every sales call—not to sell something, but to add value to customer strategy. When this happens, nothing needs to be "sold" anymore—buyers now want to buy.

—Ted Driscoll, head of sales, Americas, Nokia Software

HAVE YOU EVER TRIED TO COOK A STEW? Creating a great stew is no easy task. Many, many ingredients are required—different spices, vegetables, and meats. The combinations are endless. Interestingly, regardless of how closely you follow a recipe, no two concoctions are ever the same. But what defines a great stew is always the same. First, the aroma is engaging—its scent draws others to the kitchen. And upon sampling from the stove, the taste is savory and inviting, spawning pangs of hunger for more. Ultimately, the meal itself is flavorful, unique, and fulfilling.

If you want to make the perfect stew, you'll require a few things. First, a great stew starts with a great recipe—in other words, a game plan. Second, you'll require the proper ingredients. But surprisingly, the most important elements are a few intangibles—and these clearly show up in the finished product.

What I'm referring to is the creativity, imagination, and caring attitude of the chef.

Executing FOCAS has a lot in common with creating a great stew. First, no two FOCAS conversations are ever the same. Second, FOCAS requires a balance of thoughtful preparation, a solid game plan, and the proper mix of questions. Too much of any one ingredient—or not enough—will lead to an unpleasant aftertaste. Done well, though, it is a fulfilling experience for both creator and customer—a perfect blend that leaves both parties wanting more.

The purpose of this chapter is to help you learn FOCAS—the platinum competence of best-practices sellers. Master FOCAS and you will become a maestro at creating and concocting the only thing the customer really cares about—value stew.

To begin, let's assume you're in the process of meeting an executive for the first time. You were referred to this executive from a current customer. You subsequently phoned the executive, and after a brief discussion, she was curious enough to grant you an appointment. From your perspective, this has the earmarks of a large potential opportunity, but it will require you to create demand for your new solutions (since you suspect that your offerings would represent a new application for this organization). You've done your homework, and you show up prepared to execute your initial face-to-face discovery call.

Now let's assume you've finished your approach, and it's time to move on to your questioning phase—FOCAS. Recall that not all questions are created equal—even within the FOCAS framework. Executives especially will respond far more positively to certain types of questions, so you'll want to pay close attention to how each question category in the FOCAS model is fundamentally different from the others.

Before delving into the FOCAS model, let me mention that FOCAS is a questioning structure that leads to very dynamic customer conversations. *You would not ask these questions in a purely sequential manner.* More than likely, and when done best, you'll be skipping around, examining different areas with different FOCAS questions in a seemingly random manner. This is because one cannot predict the answers a customer will give you, and it is critical that you have a questioning mechanism that allows you to play off customer responses. *Yet, there is nothing random about how FOCAS is ultimately executed.* What keeps FOCAS on track is its strategic intent—to uncover the strategy, objectives, and challenges of the customer in a systemic way. This strategy is the glue that keeps the conversation coming back to common ground, and keeps your queries high payoff for both parties.

Last, this chapter will cover only two types of FOCAS questions—Fact and Objective. This is because each category of questions requires a fair amount of explanation. I want you to understand each question type thoroughly and will give you ample examples of each. Furthermore, each FOCAS question has a different purpose, and some are more powerful than others. For that reason, I'll cover the C-A-S of FOCAS—Concern, Anchor, and Solution Questions—in our next chapter.

FACT QUESTIONS

Most of our salespeople consider themselves customer consultants. But what we've learned was that many of our salespeople spend too much time on low-payoff open-ended questions—most of which customers find irrelevant. FOCAS helps our sales and account managers stay customer relevant. When this happens, sales happen.

—Dave Vranicar, former director, SAP/Global Business Services

Fact Questions are the easiest type of questions in the FOCAS model. As implied in the name, Fact Questions are used to collect data, facts, and information about the buyer's *current* situation. Here are some examples of common fact questions:

- Could you give me a little more background on this division?
- In which markets do you generate most of your revenue?
- What percentage of revenue is derived from your indirect distribution channel?
- How many years have you been with the company—and in this industry?

Fact Questions are necessary to capture vital information that you are unable to acquire through pre-call research. However, they are also low-payoff questions for both buyer and seller. Why? These questions do not drive discussions about either opportunities or problems—the two primary places where you can add value. Executives in particular will turn off quickly if asked too many Fact Questions. An executive's job is not to educate you on the facts of her business, so tread lightly here. You need to limit the number of Fact Questions you ask, spending five to ten minutes on them at most, and to move quickly to questions that you and the buyer find more meaningful.

Although Fact Questions offer low payoff, don't discount them. They play a necessary and important role.

- **Warm-ups:** Fact Questions are effective conversation starters when meeting someone for the first time. Think of them as softballs tossed slowly; they are a good way to get things started since they are so easy to "connect with."
- **Steering:** Fact questions also allow you to direct the conversation to the "sandbox" where you add the most value.

For instance, you may want to move a discussion from QIII: Optimization (reducing costs) to QII: Implementation (helping the customer achieve their differentiation strategy).

- **Paint by numbers:** Remember those popular books where all you had to do was color by number? In a similar vein, Fact Questions help you fill in the blanks of organizational strategy. You've got the four-quadrant schema—just use Fact Questions to help you fill in the gaps. See figure 8.1 for an example of different Fact Questions you might use depending on the quadrant of inquiry.

FIGURE 8.1: FACT QUESTIONS BY STRATEGIC QUADRANT

	Important Decisions	**Urgent Decisions**
	I Innovation Decisions	II Implementation Decisions
Blue Ocean Strategies	Could you share with me the theme of your innovations? How does innovation happen in your company—is it an organic process, or do you focus on buying smaller, innovative companies?	Tell me about some of your strategies to get your new technology quickly through its window of opportunity.
	FACT QUESTIONS	
Red Ocean Strategies	Do you still service and support customers who still use your old legacy systems?	How have growth and margins been trending in your core business over the last few years?
	IV Outsourcing Decisions	III Optimization Decisions

My Personal Hot Stove

My first job out of college was selling inexpensive laminating equipment. My boss encouraged me to always take the "high road"—call as senior as possible when prospecting. "Ask open questions that get the prospect talking," he would tell me. Unfortunately, neither of us understood that asking open-ended Fact Questions had little correlation to sales success. I was doomed—I just didn't know it yet.

Fairly quickly, I was successful in gaining an appointment with the senior vice president of marketing for a large magazine publisher. I was a rookie and was excited. I dreamed of dozens of units being sold to multiple departments!

I showed up for the appointment prepared to ask "open questions" that would get the executive to talk—traditional selling methodology. Upon being ushered into his cavernous office, I carefully explained what I did, then began my inquiry. I was in the middle of my fourth or fifth generic Fact Question when this individual cut me off curtly, stood up, pointed to the door, and told me to literally leave the premises—*now*!

He was incredulous that I was wasting his time asking him tactical questions.

I was flustered and personally embarrassed. Frankly, its sting caused me to reevaluate the wisdom of ever calling on senior executives again.

Yet I persevered and graduated from selling tabletop equipment to selling more complex systems. Unlike the inexpensive laminating equipment I used to sell, this offering was divergent and expensive—a new-to-the-market laminating system requiring a six-figure investment from customers. Selling this system would clearly require me to call on senior executives to create interest for the new concept. For me, this meant revisiting the proverbial hot stove.

Although I did achieve some success, my sales calls were essentially hit or miss endeavors. Although I was better at asking questions, they were often not the *right questions*. Many were heavily weighted in the Fact category. Many were pain based. And, my questions were always about today, lacking imagination, creativity, and vision. Looking back, it is now obvious that I never understood the perspective of the executives on whom I was calling. I thought I did, but the reality was that *my ignorance was getting in the way.*

What I now know is this: I was losing valuable opportunities to my inability to get them to communicate about their mission-critical objectives and core strategies. Quite simply, *I couldn't connect or add value to something I didn't understand.*

Years later, when I was a vice president of sales, a salesperson for a large magazine publisher came to visit. We were interested in switching all of our advertising to this publication—a fairly large investment—and she was going to make a presentation. She brought her boss. Fine. One problem—it was the same executive who had been so abrasively rude to me as a salesperson years before. Mr. Hot Stove himself.

Apparently, he was now the sales director for this particular publication. It was quickly apparent he had no recollection of our previous encounter. So what happened? Actually, nothing. I politely watched her presentation and gave her the respect she deserved (although, ironically, she essentially asked me *all* Fact Questions—the same mistake I had made years earlier when calling on her boss). As for Mr. Hot Stove, just knowing what I *could have done* was reward enough.

Summary: Fact Questions

- **Definition:** Questions that explore the facts or data of the buyer's current situation
- **Example:** "What differentiates you from your major competitors?"
- **Strategic purpose:** Uncover important background information on the company; use these questions to begin tuning into the strategic picture of the client
- **Power:** Low payoff; helps you a lot more than the executive you're talking to
- **Common mistake:** Too many, too long, and too tactical

EXERCISE

Write out some of the key Fact Questions you need to ask in your sales calls. See if you can create three Fact Questions that focus exclusively on learning about the business of the customer. An example would be, "What differentiates you from your competition?" Then create three Fact Questions that are more specific to your industry and value proposition. An example would be, "Do you currently use our category of offering?"

OBJECTIVE QUESTIONS

Objective Questions are questions used to identify and investigate the buyer's objectives. Think *opportunities*—goals, vision, and aspirations. Whereas Fact Questions uncover today's factual realities, Objective Questions get executives to explain where they are trying to go: the destination. The latter is potential, the former actual.

Objective questions are critical to helping you understand the master strategic plan of the customer, the driving goal of the questioning process. Once you learn this plan, you can drill down into each quadrant, uncovering which objectives are most critical from both a differentiation (Blue Ocean) and a productivity (Red Ocean) perspective.

Objective Questions are often simple—yet they are disarmingly powerful. Executives respond to them because most people with higher decision-making power in organizations are goal driven and have a high locus of control (a psychological term used to describe people who feel they control their own destinies). Objective Questions also help you relate to executives, the vast majority of whom live in a different time zone—the future. When you ask these questions, executives see that you're interested in their way of thinking, in joining them in their time zone.

Because Objective Questions are future focused, they correlate very strongly to successful sales outcomes.

The following are examples of Objective Questions:

- How do you see the organization needing to change over the next few years to retain its competitive edge?
- Where do you see your best future opportunities for profitable growth?
- What differentiates you from your competitors—and how do you see this separation strategy needing to change in the future? (This is a "tangled question," two questions rolled into one. The first part is actually a Fact Question, but the ending is Objective. Executives like tangled questions because they give one the creative license to go down an expanded path.)
- Could you tell me some of the things you are trying to accomplish over the next twelve months in this division?
- How do you see yourself personally evolving in the company over the next few years? Do you want to stay in human resources—or do you see a more expanded role in the enterprise one day in the future?

Four Levels of Buyer Objectives

We typically teach salespeople to look for buyer objectives at four levels, although the levels can be divided into more gradations. The four levels are as follows:

1. **Organizational objectives:** These are big picture, strategic goals often considered mission critical to the organization or a division of a large organization. For instance, the voiced objective to be "#1 in the industry within three years" is a mountaintop strategy. This mission critical strategy will

serve as a key driver behind all the objectives subsequently set in each of the four quadrants.

2. **Quadrant objectives:** These are the major goals that drive the resource spend within each of the four strategy quadrants. Every organization has separate goals for innovation, deployment, optimization, and outsourcing. You need not learn all of these goals, but you must learn the ones in the quadrants where your value proposition can best connect and add value. For instance, a QIII Objective Question might be "Do you have any key objectives for reducing the cost structure of your mature, core products?"

3. **Departmental objectives:** These are smaller picture objectives that drive the operations of individual departments. For example, every IT department in a company has two or three important objectives to accomplish annually.

4. **Personal objectives:** At times, it can be helpful to learn the personal goals of the individuals you're dealing with. These goals are best learned casually, perhaps during a walk down the hallway. For instance, you might ask, "Pat, where do you see yourself heading within the company over the next few years?" Such personal questions become easier and more appropriate to ask as relationships develop. These questions will help you better understand the motivations of the people you are working with, which can be invaluable information.

About how many Objective Questions should you ask on a typical discovery call? When is enough, enough? Although every situation is different, the rule of thumb is just a handful—perhaps two to four. Once you feel you've learned the critical goals that relate to this organization and individual, time to move on.

Objective Questions can be scaled up or down the organizational ladder, depending on the call situation. I've outlined some specific quadrant Objective Questions in figure 8.2.

Management by _____

You know the missing word in this title: *objectives*! Management by objectives (MBO) is how all contemporary leaders are trained to manage their people. Essentially, objectives are change mechanisms, created to adjust the enterprise in a manner that sustains profitable growth. Truth be told, without change, managers would not be necessary. In other words, most people know how to do their jobs without management intervention. It's the change part—often driven by objectives—that drives the need for managers.

FIGURE 8.2: OBJECTIVE QUESTIONS BY STRATEGIC QUADRANT

	Important Decisions	**Urgent Decisions**
	I Innovation Decisions	II Implementation Decisions
Blue Ocean Strategies	Do you see technology changing your industry significantly during the next three to five years? If so, how do you see yourself innovating with technology to stay ahead of the competition?	Sounds like you're ready to go to market with that new technology. Let's say it's twelve months from now and things went great. What's different for your company, and what specific goals did you accomplish?
	OBJECTIVE QUESTIONS	
Red Ocean Strategies	Do you have any key objectives for outsourcing work to outside vendors as a means to free up key people for that new project?	Sometimes just maintaining flat or slow growth is a victory in such a mature market. Could you share some of your goals in lieu of such an intensely competitive environment for your traditional, core business?
	IV Outsourcing Decisions	III Optimization Decisions

Learning the client's objectives, therefore, connects you immediately to managers who spend a great deal of time determining the best way to spend resources to achieve critical goals. Remember, if you want to learn why an organization spends resources as it does, you must start by understanding their objectives and strategies. If a senior executive thinks you have a better method to help him accomplish his critical strategies, he will find a way to work with you. Budget dollars may not be available for your solutions, but creative executives understand how to "borrow" dollars from other departments if it furthers their important initiatives.

Later in the selling cycle, you must be able to demonstrate that your offering can add value to key strategic objectives. For now, your task is simply to carefully listen and learn. Most important, you are adding value to the executive at this point with your curious inquiry. How? A bigger picture conversation about strategy is always energizing to executives as it helps them refocus on "what's really important" to the enterprise.

For sellers of complex solutions or new innovations, understanding and connecting to buyer objectives is critical. Research indicates that no connection results in no sale when demand for new, divergent offerings must be stimulated. In summary, Objective Questions in the FOCAS model enable both executives and sellers to look outside of "pain" to the other side of the value equation—opportunities and objectives.

EXERCISE

See if you can create four Objective Questions you might ask on a sales call—especially executive calls where you're attempting to understand their strategy. Create a question for each of the four objective areas (organizational, quadrant, departmental, personal). Remember, any of these questions can elicit a fairly long, intense, and fascinating discussion that helps you develop insight into organizational focus, spend, and challenges.

Summary: Objective Questions

- **Definition:** Questions that explore the objectives and opportunities of an organization, quadrant, department, or individual
- **Example:** "If you could only accomplish one or two things this year in the enterprise, what would those be?"
- **Strategic purpose:** Connection points for your value proposition; understand—and attach to—critical Blue Ocean "differentiation" and Red Ocean "productivity" objectives
- **Power:** HIGH payoff! If you can show executives a better way to accomplish mission critical objectives, you'll have a receptive audience.
- **Common mistake:** Too many pain-based questions at the expense of discussions around opportunities, objectives, vision, and differentiation

Now let's turn our attention to learning the balance of the FOCAS questioning model—a critical competence you'll need to achieve if you're to become more important to your customers. Once this happens, you'll be close to understanding how to gain a proverbial seat at the table of customer strategy.

CHAPTER NINE
FOCAS ON BUILDING A CASE FOR CHANGE

I'm interested in the perspective of the executives I'm meeting with. I'm always gauging two things: "Are we aligned" and "Do they get our value?" My time is valuable, so if they don't see value in a bigger, more strategic picture, I move on. There are plenty of senior executives and companies who need help—they just don't know it yet.

—James Dagley, vice president, channel marketing and strategy systems,
North America, Johnson Controls

A WISE PERSON ONCE TOLD ME, "People only take their own advice." Yet how often do we make the mistake of telling others what they should do—and then get frustrated when they don't follow our recommendations? The next time you feel the urge to tell someone how or why they should do something, just remember this truism: the propensity to give advice is in direct proportion to the propensity to ignore it.

If you're married or have teenage children, I'm sure you can relate.

When you make a presentation of capabilities to an executive or prospect who has not yet decided to make a change, you are directly telling that person what they should do. This violates all the tenets of human psychology. It would be better to bring to the customer table a process that ultimately makes them feel that the idea to change was theirs all along. FOCAS is such a process.

Before I finish explaining the rest of the FOCAS model, I have a confession to make. Although I've written two books on business and sales strategy, I think that business books are generally pretty boring fare. In fact, I think the best publications on business are not found in the business section at all. Instead, literature about human motivation—the psychology section—often contains fascinating and profound material on why people think and act as they do—something every salesperson should understand.

One such classic is *Human Motivation*, a thorough study by the famous behaviorist David McClelland of why people behave as they do—and how they make decisions. McClelland's research went far beyond the basics of Maslow's Hierarchy of Needs. Instead, McClelland argues that what intrinsically motivates people are four things: achievement, affinity, control, and power. Although what motivates a person is often a complex blend of all four drivers—with varying degrees of intensity—there is usually one core driver that is dominant in each personality.

Understanding human motivation is especially critical for sellers of divergent offerings who are tasked with the most challenging sale of all—*creating demand for solutions that represent a new order of things for the customer*. Creating demand is ALL about human motivation. Take, for example, selling a new technology—one that requires the buying entity to make a profound shift in how they do their work (with all the inherent angst, investment, and learning that accompanies such an endeavor). In this case, a "sale before the sale" is required—one that has nothing to do with the technology itself. Instead, the first sale requires one to construct a case for change—something best done by connecting to human desire and motivation.

Truth be told, many of the executives and people you initially call on have little interest in seeing the features and benefits associated with your product or services. No one cares about your new technology. Ironically, though, these people and executives still have psychological needs related to your offerings. What are these needs? To answer the important question, "Should we consider changing how we do our work?" Smart salespeople spend time engaging executives in conversations that help the executive answer this question—a far better strategic course than presenting the features and benefits associated with a new product or service.

FOCAS was engineered to ultimately help the people you call on answer this psychologically important question. In this manner, FOCAS meets the psychological needs of those not yet convinced of your new order of things. When used in combination with the General Recommendations step you'll learn later, you're bringing a valuable process to the executive table that helps them discover whether change might be in their best interest.

The beauty of FOCAS is that it covers both ends of the buyer motivation to change—the opportunity for gain *and* the removal of problems. We've covered the first part in some detail with the Fact and Objective questions—queries around exciting opportunities and the vision of a better future that ties to McClelland's need to achieve. Now it's time to turn our attention to Concern, Anchor, and Solution questions.

CONCERN QUESTIONS

I usually have to create demand for my total solutions, and Concern questions help me do this. I find that Concern questions really resonate at mid-levels. Assuming I then tie their challenges to my solutions, this is their motivation to adopt our technology. And senior executives who rely on these people to successfully implement our solutions appreciate me taking the time to bring these people into the decision-making fold. That means my client will get the results they expect—and that's how I generate the positive word-of-mouth so important to growing my business.

—Kim Purcell, managing director, O.C. Tanner

Concern Questions explore the dissatisfactions, difficulties, concerns, and problems that the executive or prospect may be experiencing. Therefore, the strategic intent of Concern Questions is to find buyer dissatisfaction—especially strategic discontent.

In conversations with executives, strategic dissatisfaction typically revolves around the inability to execute on strategy. For instance, executives may be frustrated by the high turnover rate in a key business unit, which is preventing the accomplishment of an important strategic initiative. Since executives are often prone to high levels of discontent with the current state, this is an important area for you to explore.

Often, the delta that separates actual (today) from potential (the future) is fertile ground for discussion (see figure 9.1). Essentially, this separation is a strategy gap that must be bridged if goals are to be reached. Closing this gap can often be challenging to executives who lack internal resources to bridge it. It is a point of perpetual dissatisfaction. If they see that you are interested in helping them close this gap, your eventual value proposition will be all the more appealing.

FIGURE 9.1: THE STRATEGY GAP

	Objective—potential
The Strategy Gap	
Current reality—actual	

Other times, Concern Questions are introduced in a more independent, isolated manner, exploring a new area where you suspect that the executive or organization may be experiencing difficulty.

Following are a few examples of Concern Questions:

- Could you share with me some of the more interesting challenges you are facing in the accomplishment of your core strategies?
- Have you had any issues with losing market share to overseas competition?
- Where does your major competitor have a decided advantage over you?
- Have you been frustrated with the degree to which you've been able to penetrate that market niche?

Concern Questions serve as an excellent foundation on which to build a case for change for your solutions. However, Concern Questions by themselves will not drive psychological change. For a senior executive to bridge the psychological divide between curiosity and commitment to your concept, two other dynamics must occur: (1) The executive must see how your solution ties to the differentiation strategy; and (2) The executive must perceive the problems you address to be systemic—and serious. That being said, Concern Questions are an excellent starting point to uncover general "constraint" areas—fruitful areas that can be sorted, sifted, and expanded in your quest to build a case for buyer change.

Very simply, in Clayton Christenson parlance, what is the "job" you want the client to hire your solutions to do? Construct your Concern Questions accordingly, exploring how effectively and efficiently this job is currently being done. You can actually construct "job buckets"—categorizing your Concern Questions under each bucket as a way to ensure a thorough discovery with an executive.

Our interviews with thousands of salespeople clearly indicate that better salespeople ask Concern Questions that resonate with executives—especially Concern Questions that *strategically tie* to the executives' objectives and opportunities. Furthermore, they ask these questions fairly early in the conversation.

Concern Questions can also be scaled up or down depending on the call situation. I've outlined some specific quadrant Concern Questions for you to look at in figure 9.2.

The biggest problem we see with the use of Concern Questions is twofold:

1. **Not enough!** Many salespeople come prepared to ask three or four Concern Questions when calling senior executives. This is woefully inadequate, kind of like forgetting to get dinner reservations for your big prom date and

FIGURE 9.2: CONCERN QUESTIONS BY STRATEGIC QUADRANT

	Important Decisions	**Urgent Decisions**
	I Innovation Decisions	II Implementation Decisions
Blue Ocean Strategies	Have you had difficulty creating a differentiation strategy that separates you from your two leading—and larger—competitors?	Hindsight is always 20/20. If you could go back and change one or two things about the deployment of your new technology six months ago, what would they be?
	CONCERN QUESTIONS	
Red Ocean Strategies	Are you frustrated that key Blue Ocean projects aren't getting done fast enough due to resources getting stuck in your traditional business?	Is the executive team under a lot of pressure to turn things around in your core markets?
	IV Outsourcing Decisions	III Optimization Decisions

subsequently ending up at a fast food joint for dinner—a very unfulfilling experience for both parties. Executives are looking for relevant, systemic, strategic conversations, and this requires thoughtful planning. At a minimum, if one views all solutions as problem-removing vehicles, one should come prepared to ask at least a dozen strategy-laden Concern Questions.

2. **Overly tactical:** Executives don't care about tactical product value. Questions about cheaper-better-faster will not resonate with busy executives who have more important issues to deal with. Bottom line? What typically separates a great Concern Question from an average one is the empathetic thought, which you will have planned long before the meeting.

Summary: Concern Questions

- **Definition:** Questions that explore the strategic constraints or problems of an organization, department, or individual
- **Example:** "What are some of the more interesting problems you face because of your position as a thought leader in your space?"
- **Strategic purpose:** Find executive dissatisfaction in multiple areas; in aggregate, these constraints help you build a case for change (especially when combined with opportunities and objectives).
- **Power:** Moderate-to-high payoff: Executives aren't interested in the pain-based "what's keeping you up at night" questions. Tie Concern Questions to their objectives and strategies and avoid tactical pain-based conversation.
- **Common mistake:** Lack of *creative, thought-provoking*, and *strategic* concern questions. These questions need to be

carefully considered and prepared. Give their creation the thought the executive you are calling on deserves.

ANCHOR QUESTIONS

My salespeople used to jump to solutions whenever they found a customer problem. No more. Today, we mutually examine with a client the real consequences of a problem—determining whether it's even worthwhile for either of us to explore. This makes much better use of both of our time and the executives we call on. These questions really help you gain traction.

—Milan Dayalal, vice president of sales, Dakota Software Systems

Finding executive discontent through good Concern Questions is important. However, as we mentioned a moment ago, finding this discontent won't be enough to get commitment from the executive to undergo change. To generate intellectual traction will require the use of a different type of FOCAS question— Anchor Questions. These questions are especially powerful—so have one more cup of coffee so you can pay extra close attention to this critical section.

Anchor Questions explore the seriousness of problems already identified. These areas of dissatisfaction will most likely be unearthed when you are asking Objective or Concern questions. But Anchor Questions are designed to broaden the discussion of these issues, helping an executive see that narrow problems often have systemic consequences. For this reason, Anchor Questions are extremely high payoff because they help executives see the broader—or enterprise—implications of a problem.

Examples of Anchor Questions include, among others:

- Do you feel that your bottlenecking problem is affecting your reputation in the market?
- How is that void in hiring quality people affecting your ability to make faster inroads into the new market?
- Are you concerned that your layoffs are affecting the quality of service you provide customers?
- Sounds like you're frustrated about the amount of time your salespeople are spending responding to RFPs and RFQs that have a low probability of success. What important sales work isn't getting done as a result of this?

I've outlined some specific quadrant Anchor Questions for you to look at in figure 9.3.

Systemic Consequences

Anchor Questions are second in power behind Objective Questions within the FOCAS model. These questions resonate because they represent the reasoning process of an executive. In other

FIGURE 9.3: ANCHOR QUESTIONS BY STRATEGIC QUADRANT

	Important Decisions	Urgent Decisions
	I Innovation Decisions	II Implementation Decisions
Blue Ocean Strategies	Do you think the lack of a differentiation strategy is ultimately going to cost you more market share?	How has your failure to sell your "total solutions" impacted your ability to secure budgeting for the hiring of new, key people?
	ANCHOR QUESTIONS	
Red Ocean Strategies	If key people are getting stuck in your core business, do you think that will delay the launch time of your new technology solutions?	If margins keep deteriorating in your core business, will this cause you to take more drastic cost-cutting measures?
	IV Outsourcing Decisions	III Optimization Decisions

words, senior executives are taught to look at the whole system. Their job is to anticipate the consequences of a problem on the entire enterprise. In areas where strategy is not being executed properly, the systemic implications can be significant.

Problems rarely exist in a vacuum or silo. Rather, problems are usually like dominoes—creating a potential negative chain reaction often unconsidered by the executive. That chain reaction runs through the organization and through the strategies for the organization. As a simple example, consider how the problem of not enough resources—people and capital—in one department or division might affect other areas of an enterprise. This problem is being caused by overfeeding the Red Ocean core business, which sets off a chain reaction as follows:

Implication 1: Key managers are frustrated by their inability to quickly launch the new initiative.

Implication 2: This causes delays in getting the new differentiated offering to be embraced by customers.

Implication 3: This causes the market to question the validity of the new application.

Implication 4: This causes the board of directors to be alarmed.

Implication 5: This adversely affects the morale and motivation of the organization and support for the new vision.

Each implication in the chain reaction must be included in a discussion of the true cost and weight of a problem: in this case, resources getting stuck in the Red Ocean core business. True consultative salespeople recognize—and help buyers recognize, when necessary—the systemic consequences of a found problem by using Anchor Questions to tie together all of the associated implications.

Unfortunately, this is an area where salespeople typically lack effectiveness. As you'll see, salespeople are often anxious to rush in with solutions to any found problem. This may work when selling small offerings but will not generate positive traction with senior executives who would prefer *not* to get dragged into the tactical abyss. In other words, jumping in with solutions too early means one is solving problems for people who aren't interested in solutions. Nothing will kill a sales opportunity faster.

Done properly, Anchor Questions help executives see the "bigness" of a situation. This gives an opportunity the potential to live. Most important, Anchor Questions help tie strategic quadrants together by tying constraints to a larger strategic picture. For instance, let's assume you've found the classic QIII (Red Ocean/optimization) issue of deteriorating profit margins. By asking an Anchor Question such as "How are deteriorating margins in your core line affecting investment in your new brand?" you've ultimately tied the QIII problem to a potentially more serious QII problem (Blue Ocean/deployment). This dialogue is strategic, crosses quadrant boundaries, and helps divergent opportunities gain important momentum.

The Fork in the Road: Which Path Is Best?

Anchor Questions assume a problem has been found. Although the initial reaction of salespeople may be to jump in with solutions, savvy salespeople know when it is time to "drop an anchor." The strategic intent of Anchor Questions is to *grow* dissatisfaction—and therefore demand for a solution—systemically. Remember, executives will not commit to change until dissatisfaction is thought to be systemically serious.

This is the proverbial fork in the road that sellers often face. In other words, once a problem is uncovered, should one suggest a solution or explore how the problem may be impacting the organization in other, more serious, ways? The road less traveled is to Anchor, and it is the road that will assuredly lead to more successful sales outcomes. Research proves this beyond measure.

If solutions are introduced too early, before the executive sees the enterprise connection, the executive will object. And, assuredly, objections are not good. In fact, research shows that there are seven times as many buyer objections in a failed sales outcome as there are in a successful sales outcome. This goes against sales folklore that suggests all executive objections are good things. Experienced salespeople know the truth—resistance is best dealt with by making sure it does not occur in the first place.

To keep the discussion focused on the bigness of the problem, be sure to

1. Use Concern Questions to find strategic dissatisfaction areas.
2. Avoid the impulse to try to solve the buyer's problems or remove the dissatisfaction areas.
3. Use Anchor Questions to grow systemic dissatisfaction.

Following is an example of how an Anchor Question might be used.

Concern Questions to find problems and dissatisfactions	Executive's response indicating the presence of a problem	Anchor Questions to explore the implications of the found problem
Have you had any difficulties gaining traction with customer executives for your new differentiated value proposition?	Yes. We're generating a lot of interest, but not enough signed orders so far.	Is this causing your people to question the validity of the new value proposition?
		How is this delay affecting your ability to make further investments required to ultimately make this strategy a success?

Anchor Questions are extremely high payoff. After Objective Questions, they most closely correlate to sales success. Yet most salespeople ask few, if any, Anchor Questions. As a result, they fail to get to the next appointment or next step. They fail to move problems from the back burner ("we can live with this") to the front burner ("perhaps this problem is serious enough to consider"). Without question, Anchor Questions should be viewed as a differentiator between top and average salespeople.

We see it continuously, so it bears repeating: Average salespeople continually jump in with solutions when they find pain. Better salespeople, instead, grow strategic dissatisfaction by helping executives see the systemic consequences to found problems.

Summary: Anchor Questions

- **Definition:** Questions that explore the systemic consequences of a found problem; they broaden discussions

- **Example:** "Are you concerned that negative publicity in that area might affect your stock price?"
- **Strategic purpose:** Connecting to strategy means helping executives connect the dots. Anchor questions grow dissatisfaction by broadening discussions into other strategic areas that might be negatively impacted.
- **Power:** HIGH payoff! After objective questions, these questions most closely correlate to sales success. Senior executives think in terms of the big, broad picture—the intent behind Anchor Questions. This makes them especially powerful with executives.
- **Common mistake:** Impulsive salespeople who feel the urgency to rush in with solutions at the mention of any problem by the executive. Consequently, conversations that lack Anchor Questions are the major error. A strategic conversation cannot be strategic if Anchor Questions are omitted. The preferred alternative is to patiently build a case for change by thoughtfully broadening the strategic discussion with Anchor Questions.

EXERCISE

Think of all your products and services as problem-removing vehicles. Now, list the top four problems you feel that your offerings solve for an executive you might call on. For each problem, see if you can create two Anchor Questions that help the executive explore whether this problem might be leading to other, more-serious problems.

SOLUTION QUESTIONS

A few Solution Questions can really help determine whether you're making progress in the discovery process. It's almost like a tire gauge, helping our sales directors understand whether the buyer might be ready for solutions—or not. There is nothing worse than solving problems for people who aren't looking for solutions, and Solution Questions help you avoid this natural sales impulse.

—Nathalie Petri, regional sales manager, Visual Marking Systems

Finally, the last question in the FOCAS model is Solution Questions. Solution Questions are unique in that they develop the executive's recognition of the value or usefulness of your solution. Unlike Concern or Anchor questions, they do not explore dissatisfaction areas. Rather, these are value-focused questions that help you understand the interest level of an executive in potential solutions.

Following are a few examples of Solution Questions:

- In what ways might it help your organization to solve that bottleneck issue?
- How would it help you if we could free up valuable resources in that area?
- What type of economic impact might it have if you could reduce turnover?
- When I return, what type of solutions would you like me to focus on?

I've tied Solution Questions to the strategy matrix shown in figure 9.4.

Solutions Questions can also help expand the buyers' perspective of value. For example, an executive may be curious about using your company for outsourcing solutions but may not have tied that value to freeing up resources that could be redeployed

FIGURE 9.4: SOLUTION QUESTIONS BY STRATEGIC QUADRANT

	Important Decisions	**Urgent Decisions**
	I Innovation Decisions	II Implementation Decisions
Blue Ocean Strategies	Would you see a brainstorming session focused on innovation—something we call a technology road map—as helpful?	Do you think an outside perspective on your ability to sell new innovation would be useful?
		SOLUTION QUESTIONS
Red Ocean Strategies	Would you be interested in ideas that might help you free up your resources to redeploy more important areas of the business?	In what other ways might a productivity analysis of you core operations add value?
	IV Outsourcing Decisions	III Optimization Decisions

for Blue Ocean purposes. Good Solution Questions help people see these value connections.

What ties these questions together is that each forces the buyer to discuss the potential value of your solutions, which makes them ideal to ask at the very end of your sales calls—before you potentially waste time creating solution propositions in which the prospect may have little interest. We've always felt that in a discovery call, a salesperson is buying as much as selling. By this we mean that a salesperson is evaluating the opportunity and deciding if it's worthwhile to invest more time and resources into it. Solution Questions should help you make this determination.

Solution Questions are value based. In effect, they help you learn whether the executive sees value in the removal of problems. For that reason, they are more optimistic in tone, unlike the dissatisfaction focus of Concern and Anchor questions. Solution Questions get the buyer to think about potential solutions

...werful in your goal to gain psycho-
...executives on whom you are calling.
...in a seat at the table, and you'll need
...that seat but also to get on the *same*
...prospect. When that happens, things

and determine whether or not their problems or dissatisfactions are serious enough to justify action. On the flip side, they also help the buyer see your potential role in the achievement of their objectives and opportunities and help you get feedback on the value of helping in important strategic areas.

Solution Questions clearly have a dark side, though. Used too early in a conversation, they can be a sure death knell. Questions like "If I could show you a way to . . . would you be interested?" are transparent and manipulative—and will brand you immediately as a *salesperson* (ouch!). This will negate any progress you made with the executive in establishing yourself as a *businessperson who sells*. All your hard work will disappear down the drain. Remember, the key with Solution Questions is timing.

Summary: Solution Questions

- **Definition:** Questions that explore the value of a potential solution
- **Example:** "Would it be helpful if we could help reduce turnover in that division?"
- **Strategic purpose:** Determining whether the executive sees value in a potential solution; similar to tipping your toe in the water—does the other person see value here?
- **Power:** Moderate, at best. Helpful, but use carefully; best to use at the very end of a strategic conversation, after summarizing what you've heard
- **Common mistake:** Salespeople, especially the product myopic, use these questions ad nauseam. Many salespeople also mistakenly use these as trial close questions, leaving a very bad aftertaste in the executive's mouth. Last, when used early in the conversation, they are especially transparent.

WHAT HAPPENS AFTER FOCAS?

Congratulations—you're done asking your FOCAS questions. You've learned a great deal about the strategies, opportunities, and problems of this organization. Best of all, you didn't do any "selling." You didn't even mention any of your products or solutions—except when you gave the initial overview of the company. So please, give yourself a big gold star for that accomplishment.

Now what happens?

Remember, discovery, this initial meaningful conversation, is the most critical sales process step when dealing with senior executives. When executed properly, demand for new concepts and solutions are stimulated. As I've outlined, discovery has four components that assist the seller in executing an effective call strategy: approach (90 seconds); FOCAS questioning (30 to 120 minutes); summary (1 minute); and recommendations (30 seconds). Each component is a unique *skill*.

So now that the FOCAS stage is complete, simply summarize your conversation and recommend the next steps—the last two parts of the discovery. The following is a good example of how to do that.

Pat, thanks for your time today. Let me tell you what I'm hearing. What I've heard you say is that you have some key goals here, here, and here, but that you're experiencing some significant challenges over here, here, and here. Did I get that right?

Assuming Pat says yes, that you got it right, here's what you say next:

mechanism is incredibly p
logical alignment with the
I promised to help you g
this step not only to gai
side of the table as you
start getting really fun.

d
like
you
come
relevan
compan

Secon
and Beth
they were t
in some of th
lenges. I think
relevant and v
that?

And, that's it. You'

I cannot emphasize enoug
tency like FOCAS. Withou
this nature, you will not be
that build trust and credibilit
you must actually connect you
gies. This next step is called (

CHAPTER TEN

ON THE SAME SIDE
OF THE TABLE

When I'm in a meeting, and our salesperson is being introduced by the customer as a "consultant or adviser," I know this person is doing the job. That means that this person is no longer perceived as a salesperson. When this shift happens, trust and credibility go way up. We are now on the same side of the table with customers— brainstorming, answering questions, and suggesting ideas. At that point, the question is no longer "if" our two organizations are going to work together—but when and how.

—John T. Stuart, national sales director, Genentech USA

FROM MY PERSPECTIVE, THERE IS NOTHING as fulfilling as sitting on the same side of the table as the client, working together toward an important common vision. But how does one get to that point in a client relationship when you become one team, not two? When do typical, under-optimized relationships turn into something more meaningful, powerful, and valuable for both parties?

Without sounding overly simplistic, the tool you will learn in this chapter will help you do just that. By the very end of this pivotal step—the General Recommendations—you will be suggesting ideas and options that allow you to showcase the value you have to offer. You'll create mini-offerings that simultaneously advance your selling cycle toward a positive conclusion. Best of all, *you'll be getting paid* for these important services—creative progressions that smart salespeople suggest to clients as ways to shorten long selling cycles and to advance relationships. But these value-adding steps won't be embraced unless a proper connection to customer strategy has first been established.

BRIDGING THE DIVIDE

Remember, *you* set up the first meeting with the client; the executive did not call you. This means that you will need to create demand, not only with this executive but also with all those executives and managers with an important voice in this decision. You are off to a good start with your first discovery meeting—an initial connection was made through a *business conversation* relevant to both parties. You've set a date for the second meeting, and the executive has invited a few more people to attend—other executives and/or managers who clearly have a voice in the decision you are trying to shape. The table is set—now what?

Good strategy is always based on sound objectives, so let's start by examining some important goals you'll want to ideally accomplish on this next visit.

1. **The case for change:** You need to demonstrate that change might be in the best interest of the client—at least worthy of further investigation. We'll explore this in more detail later in the chapter.
2. **Same side of table:** At some point during this second meeting, those in attendance must begin seeing you as a consultant. Early in the meeting, they will not see you this way. But

if this call is executed properly, you'll gradually see signs of a perception shift. This shift can manifest itself in different ways—from a spike in interest and energy levels to a new respect or deference in the tone of their questions.

3. **Shock absorber:** The goal here is to not do anything overly disruptive that might kill a perfectly good opportunity, yet still get the buyer to "put skin on the table" in a way that advances the cycle forward. In other words, you need a shock absorber mechanism between *needs analysis* (the discovery call) and your eventual *specific proposal* (in the future).

4. **Conceptual agreement:** The sooner you can conceptually agree on *direction*, the better. When I say *direction*, I mean a shared vision in which the customer is, at a minimum, willing to dip their collective toe in the water to determine validity. Remember, you don't want to spend a large amount of time and resources chasing change-resistant rabbits. To determine whether they are committed, get answers to the following questions:

   o Are they willing to take *real risk* by sticking their necks out and committing to a small next step?

   o Can they make *real bets*, or do you need to get in front of another group of executives?

   o Do they "get" your *real value*, or do they see vendors as vendors, someone to wring the lowest price out of, not grasping your true unique value?

Ultimately, you want to paint a vision for the prospect—a powerful vision that adds significant value to their current strategy. This happens *after* you've demonstrated that you understand their objectives and constraints, but *before* showing ideas and options. In other words, a vision is only introduced after one has *connected to strategy*.

So, how do you go about achieving these goals? How do you build your vision for change? Many salespeople backslide at this point in the sales cycle to pushing products and solutions when they should be focusing on connecting to and enhancing customer strategy. Here are a few tactics you might think are appropriate for the second meeting you've so skillfully arranged. Let me tell you, they are not.

- **A presentation of capabilities:** This familiar presentation is your dog and pony show—your corporate capabilities, range of solutions, advantages and benefits, and examples of customers who were wise enough to invest in your offerings. There certainly is a time and place for this type of presentation—unfortunately, not for this particular second call scenario. I've already explained why this type of presentation won't work in a first meeting with executives. It still won't work. Why? Because you haven't built a case for change yet. If you try this approach, eventually the costs of change will be examined—change costs that far exceed the capital investment you are asking for, such as management time, resistance from the old guard, disruption of the daily business, down time to train, and distraction from other key initiatives. When these costs are considered, the group that was originally so enthusiastic about your solutions will decide to sit this one out.

- **Additional discovery:** Additional discussion of goals and constraints should be part of this call—but definitely not the strategy that will *drive* the call. The people attending the meeting will want to hear some value: remember, you're the entertainment from their boring business day. You promised your initial contact that you would return with some ideas and options; if you don't deliver, you'll seem unprepared and unknowledgeable about their business and yours.

- **Specific proposal:** To actually quote or propose a total solution at this point would be a major turnoff for all involved. It might look good on your forecast sheet in the short term, but your 75 percent probability rate will quickly crash to zero in a matter of weeks. Remember, the executive you met in the first meeting was not in shopping mode for solutions. Therefore, the collective psychological needs of this group do not revolve around which is the best solution option. Instead, they need to be convinced that changing how things are done will benefit them.

On a side note, there is a time and place for a presentation of capabilities early in the sales cycle—when you are selling to a buyer who is at the shopping stage, is actively looking for a solution, and needs to see how your offerings stack up. If you want to better understand customer decision-making models—the psychology of how executives and customers make risk/reward decisions—I encourage you to read my first book, *Selling Is Dead*. Best-practices sellers always base call strategy on where the customer is in his decision-making process. I would encourage you to pick up a copy if you don't use such models as a basis for creating strategy for each selling opportunity you engage.

BUILDING A CASE FOR CHANGE

What stimulates change? Barring traumatic events that bind people together into action, it is extremely difficult to get a group of people to embrace a new order of things. But quite often, a simple glance in the mirror serves to plant the original seeds of change. This is especially true when the reflection is compared with what could be, the ideal state. Reflection may cause one to realize that current strategies are too small when compared to large objectives.

Consequently, one of the most important tools you can bring to the client table is a "mirror" that forces honest reflection on the current reality—a presentational reflection that helps the group better envision their situation. The captured snapshot contrasts two essential pieces of information: client objectives, constraints, and current processes contrasted against best practices—that is, your vision of *their better future.*

This presentation is meant to help the audience arrive at the conclusion that change may be in their best interest. Your discourse is meant to reflect the current client situation—key objectives, strategies, and constraints. A new vision for the future may be suggested within this presentation—one that is consistent with customer objectives but suggests a superior strategic path to accomplishment.

In this change presentation, specific solutions are rarely discussed. Solutions are like DNA—one-of-a-kinds—and it would not be appropriate to venture down this advice path without a far better understanding of customer needs. The point here is not to avoid a discussion of a solution, but to focus the discussion where it most belongs—on the real psychological needs of this decision base.

Change is the first sale an advisor must make when attempting to create demand with people who work in environments that are naturally inclined to the status quo. And the way to make that sale is with General Recommendations.

GENERAL RECOMMENDATIONS

The General Recommendations tool will enable you to connect to customer strategy, build a case for change, and achieve your other goals for this second meeting. The purpose of this tool is to establish a business argument that change is in the customer's best interest. Done properly, this mechanism not only accomplishes this goal but also offers a range of options for how to move forward at appropriate—but varying—risk levels.

All buyers love options. Here is a simple example. Let's say you were in the market for a plasma widescreen television. Unquestionably, you would want to look at all the major options before making this important buying decision. If your investigation started with a large club store that only had one or two brand choices, you would move on to establishments that allowed you to look at other alternatives.

Remember, you do not sell to organizations—you sell to people. And, people like options. It's that simple. General Recommendations give buyers creative alternatives—ideally three options that represent logical commitment levels. Underscore *commitment* here, for there can be no real relationship without it.

Keep in mind that General Recommendations are structured to keep the discussion focused on *business*—not *offerings*. The latter is truly the lowest common denominator for the executives and managers with whom you are engaged, unless they are in the shopping stage, have budgeted for your offering, and are actively looking for alternatives. Again, this is an entirely different scenario requiring a vastly different strategy.

General Recommendations are presented in a document that you will walk through with the buyer, page by page. This can be done in a visual presentation format for a larger group, but since your second meeting usually will have only a handful of individuals, a paper document is more appropriate. The process of delivering the document is critical, and the delivery should become a disciplined skill. I'll discuss this more in a moment.

A General Recommendations document consists of five parts:

1. Situation Summary
2. Goals and Objectives
3. Constraints, Issues, and Challenges
4. Vision
5. Options

Again, General Recommendations are the ideal next step *after* you have learned the objectives, opportunities, and constraints of the organization through discovery. If you lack this information, then you're not ready to deliver General Recommendations. That's okay. Just contact the executive or an associate of this person for the information required to fill in the strategic gaps. Do not, *under any circumstance,* return with a change document that has gaping holes.

Inch by Inch Everything Is a . . .

How do you introduce the General Recommendations document? After doing your approach for the benefit of the individuals who were not present at the discovery meeting, you'll describe the purpose of your visit in a manner similar to the following:

And, again, thanks for meeting today. As promised, I've spent some time thinking about your business and shared your situation with a few of my associates for their thoughts. Based on that, I've documented some of the important information you shared with me at our last meeting. I've also included some ideas and options that I believe might add value to your situation.

If it's okay with you, I'd like to hand out this document one page at a time. This may seem a bit unusual, but it will keep everyone on the same page—literally—to ensure the most efficient use of your time. Is that okay?

This step-by-step sequence is essential. It ensures that each page of the General Recommendations is given the proper attention necessary to build sufficient psychological momentum toward change. You don't want the group to lose focus by flipping ahead—often to the Options section. And by asking approval to hand out your document one step at a time, you'll avoid any resistance to this process.

An unwise strategy may be to hand out a bound document. Resist this natural urge at all costs. If you do this, you can only hope that everyone in the meeting follows your advice to stay on the same page. As someone with a short attention span (borderline ADD), I can vouch that many similarly wired businesspeople will ignore your directions, lose complete impulse control, and jump immediately ahead. When this happens, the game is over.

An important consequence of staying on the same page is the spirited discussion that often ensues within the group. This occurs frequently. When it happens, you are no longer selling, but are facilitating a discussion. This is an ideal scenario. Interest level and energy are raised when people are active participants. Sidebars often flare up, but if this happens, it is another positive clue that you're gaining intellectual traction.

Accountability to Change

Facilitation of a discussion about change is not only fun, it also creates accountability. Peer groups play the ultimate role in whether change will or will not happen. This is one reason why it is critical for you to get additional people to the second meeting. If your second meeting is one-on-one with the same executive, "no" is any easy alternative. There is no accountability.

But, when a group of peers and associates all agree that problems are serious—and strategies should be shifted—accountability to change occurs. The herd moves. In other words, individuals rarely go against the consensus of their peers for fear of being ostracized. This is an extremely powerful dynamic in how change occurs in organizations, and this is part of the power of the General Recommendations step.

SECTION I: SITUATION SUMMARY

This first section of the General Recommendations document contains factual information learned via your Fact Questions during the discovery. No more than one page in length, it quickly summarizes data such as the following:

- Core or existing product and/or service offerings
- New innovations/products/services
- Uniqueness and history of the company
- Target market focus/niche
- Trends or emerging patterns

The situation summary is not the place to list any objectives or problems. Save that for the next sections. As for structure, I usually document in paragraph format, although others prefer bullet point format. Either way works.

Hand out this single sheet. Let the meeting attendees read it quickly, get agreement that you've got your facts correct, and ask the members of the buying organization if any key facts have been left out. Then move on. Unless this group is either inebriated (two martini lunch?) or illiterate (not highly probable), please do *not* read this document out loud for the participants. Instead, allow them a few minutes to read through this page in silence before inquiring if you accurately depicted the facts of the situation.

There is no reason to dwell here—these are just low-payoff facts. What this section will demonstrate, though, is that you listened, learned, and have a conceptual grasp of the business.

SECTION II: GOALS AND OBJECTIVES

The Goals and Objectives section is the first real pivot point of the meeting. This portion of the document ideally captures the critical objectives of the enterprise at two levels: organizational and departmental. Please do not confuse their organizational goals with objectives related to your specific product/service. These are two very different things, and your job is to capture the former only.

Examples you might document include the following:

Blue Ocean Objectives
- By end of year, establish an ISO Certified Program in the new division
- Grow new platform sales to $10 million in a new vertical market
- Sell 25 percent more services—a key indicator of your transition to total solutions

Red Ocean Objectives

- Implement new technology to reduce service labor in the core business
- Reduce cost structure in operations by 3 percent
- Begin using outsourcing as a mechanism to reduce cost

How did you originally find out about these important objective areas? By asking Objective Questions, the most critical questions in the FOCAS structure, during the discovery process.

There are two very important reasons why you must document customer objectives. First, you send a very powerful message—that you are a *businessperson*. You will often hear an executive comment, "You really listened." This is when your brand begins to shift with the group. Second, by documenting critical goals, you imply that you can help in these areas, and that raises attention levels.

Again, additional people have joined this meeting who were not privy to the information discussed in the initial discovery. Consequently, you'll learn of other key goals not previously discussed. In other words, after the group has read the objectives you've listed, ask these new individuals if they have any goals or objectives they would like to add? This often generates important information and discussion.

As a rule of thumb, the Goals and Objectives section is presented in a fairly short period of time. On different occasions, though, it can stimulate some interesting—and often lengthy—dialogue. The time element is insignificant, whether five or fifty minutes. The important point is that this section positions you as someone who can simplify complexity. In other words, you sifted, sorted, and filtered through a tremendous amount of data, and condensed key objectives on one sheet of paper. Not bad! You're gaining trust and credibility, and a few members of this group are now thinking you might be able to add value to their enterprise.

SECTION III: CONSTRAINTS, ISSUES, AND CHALLENGES

This next pivotal section of the General Recommendations mechanism reveals the problems—and the systemic consequences of those problems—originally uncovered in your discovery visit. These issues should be listed on a single page. A bullet-point layout often works best.

Below are some examples of constraints that one might list.

- The business is losing market share to overseas competition at a rate of 2 percent per year. Low-cost foreign manufacturers have also led to price pressure and commoditization.
- Selling new products and innovations, which represent higher margin potential, has been a major struggle for the sales and marketing team.
- Some turnover during the past twelve months within the leadership ranks has caused some disruption. Filling two of these key positions remains a challenge.

If you prefer, you can categorize your questions under specific headers. For instance, note that I categorized objectives as either Blue or Red Ocean. You could do the same here, perhaps using different constraint categories (organizational, departmental, etc.). Since every organization is different and every set of constraints is different, I'll leave you to sort that one out.

Again, I would suggest listing all constraints on one page only. But list as many as possible—something salespeople think is difficult but is actually quite easy. If you can think of only three or four, just think of the consequences of one of the problems you already listed as a means to document more.

For instance, let's look at the first constraint on the list to see how this works: The business is losing market share to overseas competition at a rate of 2 percent per year. Low-cost foreign manufacturers have also led to price pressure and commoditization.

Now, based on that issue, how many negative consequences can you think of that might systemically affect the enterprise? Think about this for a moment. Can you see how many other problems this single constraint might cause this organization? This issue might lead to the following problems:

- Decreasing profit margins
- Pressure on the stock price if a publicly held firm
- Owner frustration with current management if privately held
- Weakened ability to attract new talent to the firm

The key is to help the client see that their problems have systemic implications. You are attempting to broaden the discussion at this point, and this document gives you the perfect vehicle to accomplish this strategy.

When discussing each documented concern or issue, *suppress* the impulse to offer solutions. Again, as mentioned earlier, use thoughtful (meaning preplanned) Anchor Questions that broaden discussions even further. Your questions might sound like these:

- "Tom (vice president of human resources), you weren't at the last meeting, and I was curious if some of the recent layoffs in the core business were affecting morale or turnover in other areas?"

- "Michelle (regional sales manager), has the negative publicity generated from the layoffs made it difficult for your salespeople to gain traction in the new key market?"

The key here is to come prepared with appropriate Concern and Anchor questions that can help you find and grow additional strategic dissatisfaction. This will often lead to a very robust discussion—and some passionate, but healthy, arguments from those most affected in the room.

Here's an important point to keep in mind. The constraints that you documented—and that are being discussed by those in this meeting—are not your problems. The customer "owns" these problems, serious or otherwise. This is your attitude and role—an impartial third party facilitating a discussion. I often tell the executives I meet that until they pay me, they get to keep their problems. I do this half in jest, but it sends an important message that their problems will persist until they decide to *commit* to change.

You're so very close to the finish line, I feel like I need to give you a shout of encouragement. Ready? You are the best! Anyone, and I mean anyone, who has lasted this far is a very special person. You are in the minority of your profession, so congratulations. Now get ready for the last two sections!

SECTION IV: VISION

The Vision section is where you paint the end-game picture for your client. This should be a fairly simple but powerful depiction of the better future you are espousing for this particular client.

What is this end-game vision? To answer that, you must first answer Peter Drucker's profound question. At his death at ninety-three years of age, Drucker was considered the greatest business thinker of his generation. He was brilliant in his ability to simplify very complex concepts—a sage similar to Warren Buffett. Drucker's favorite question for businesspeople was, What business are you in? It's the type of elegantly simple and profound question that all businesspeople struggle to answer in a clear, crisp manner.

For our purposes, how you answer this question often determines the vision statement you will communicate to the prospect. Yet this can be very difficult for individuals to articulate since they are so very close to their businesses. And the closer you are to a business, the more maddening this challenge of clear articulation becomes.

Let me give you an example. My company, Sogistics, does a tremendous amount of sales training. But we are not in the sales training business. This might seem strange to say since we actually generate a large percentage of our revenues from training.

Instead, I think of Sogistics as a numerator company, helping companies grow faster and more profitably by building sales teams that can truly make bigger customer difference.

When we share a vision with a client, it usually revolves around that last line. This is what we want to help them do—create a sales team that can differentiate their organization by simply helping their customers differentiate. We live and breathe it; you probably have a similar passion for your business. The point is that if you cannot articulate what business you are in, then you need to get to this "naked essence" as soon as possible. If you just can't seem to put it together in a way that gets to the real core, simply ask your best customers. Often, they can clearly see what business you are really in.

When you share your vision of a better client future in a short statement, you are a leader. And in a bold, but polite, manner, you're asking them whether they want to lead, follow, or tell you to get out of the way. Ultimately, it is their choice. But the fact that you have shared a vision that aligns with their current strategy will now make this next section very interesting for all involved.

From a documentation perspective, this is often nothing more than a few short paragraphs. In my estimation, the shorter and more succinct, the better. In addition to articulating your vision for the client—a vision your solutions will drive—you must now connect your vision to their strategy. This may be no more than a paragraph or a few short sentences, but it is essential that you articulate this connection.

The following is a vision we might suggest to a potential client. I've italicized the specific areas where we've tied our suggested partnering vision to the client strategy.

> Our vision is to help ABC company build a strategic sales and account-management team that customers find relevant, valuable, and strategically impactful. This vision is more than a tactic: it is a strategic imperative requiring a strong commitment from the top leadership of your organization. Our joint goal is to develop the type of "businesspeople who sell," who can connect and add value to customer strategy. *Since a critical goal for your company is to create more total solutions relationships—bigger, longer-lasting partnerships with customers—senior leadership support is critical in this transition.*
>
> From our perspective, this vision ties strongly into the "customer intimate" strategy of your company. Better market facing enables customer relationships based more on results than products—a stated objective of your CEO. A transformation of this nature would also

enable your company to separate and differentiate from cheaper-priced competitors—another stated goal of your organization. Delivering strategic customer results is an extremely difficult value proposition to imitate, as it is based on the knowledge of your people rather than any single product or service.

This is the expressed partnering vision of our relationship—to help you build the most productive sales and account management team in your industry, one that wins and wins more often for the simple reason that it understands how to add more value to the customer's bottom line.

SECTION V: OPTIONS

Now the fun part. It's time to present creative options that get the real ball rolling. As a strategic advisor, your job is to create and capture customer value. Yet value should never be used in the singular. Some combination of value always exists in any solution or option, but it is impossible to quantify the exact proportion of each that drives any given decision.

That said, by offering fundamentally different types of value at this point, you can better—and more quickly—determine the true quality of this opportunity.

Here are a few important notes.

- When writing the Options section of a General Recommendations document, you should not present more than three options. Three is ideal—two is usually not enough, four is too many and confusing.
- Only one option should be written on a page. This is important for several reasons. First, if you give the members of

the buying team multiple options at once, they will read ahead. This is a self-inflicted wound you can easily avoid by following the proper protocol of one option per page. Trust me on this one; battling executive attention deficit disorder (EADD) is no fun.

- A brief description of each option is all that is necessary on each page. Do not go into detail. General Recommendations are meant to be just that—*general*. If interest is expressed in a specific option, you can supply a detailed proposal later. This is an important mind-set to adhere to, that the purpose is to gain *conceptual agreement* on direction, not bog the meeting down with minutiae.

- *Never* list pricing, but always tell your prospect the "price of poker" for an option—before they ask. In other words, just give them a round number on the cost of an option if they express interest, explaining that you can supply a detailed quotation later if they are actively interested. Better to round the general investment figure you verbally quote up rather than down. By doing so, you're anticipating some negotiation down the road, and this strategy gives you some wiggle room should the buyer decide to negotiate a better price with you at a later date.

- After each option is discussed, gauge the reaction of the key people in the meeting. This can be done with nonthreatening Solution Questions, such as "Do you think this option might be helpful?" or "How do you think this option would impact your ability in that area?" Executives are very candid people who typically call it as they see it. Also, don't become emotionally invested in any of these options. If you do, you'll turn back into that creature you've been trying to avoid—a traditional salesperson. Remember, your purpose is to help these people, so if they don't see value in any particular option, your attitude must be "no problem." At a minimum, an immediate no on all options (this doesn't happen very often) will save you from wasting valuable time later chasing those elusive rabbits.

Where the Puck Is

Remember Wayne Gretzky? Some consider him the greatest player in the history of hockey. When asked what differentiated him from other players, he would answer, "I never skated to where the puck was—I skated to where the puck was going to be." Your Options Strategy within General Recommendations is analogous to Wayne Gretzky. Don't think where the buyer is at the beginning of the General Recommendations meeting. Rather, think where the buyer will be psychologically by the end of this General Recommendations call. When done properly, buyer psychology changes from "curious to committed" through this process, and some of your options need to reflect this anticipated psychological change.

Essentially, there are three major types of options that you might include in your General Recommendations document. They include Demand Creation Options, Service Demand Options, and Risk Mitigation Options. Let's briefly discuss each type.

Demand Creation Options

Demand Creation Options are meant to help those who must decide whether change is in their best interest. These options, if selected, seek to help answer this important question. An example of a Demand Creation Option is to conduct an analysis or study in your field of expertise. These in-depth looks might be called many things: perhaps a "functional analysis" or a "productivity study." An analysis can be highly formal or intensively detailed. Your organization might actually have the capability to generate multiple types of these demand-creation analytics.

Why would a buyer agree to do a study of this nature? The answer is simply because buyers appreciate an outside opinion on how they stack up to best practices. In other words, they want to know how they are doing compared to their competition. A study—and the subsequent findings report—gives them a yardstick in this pursuit.

Service Demand Options

Service Demand Options are ideally suited for buyers who have active needs. In other words, these are shopping-stage buyers who may have budgeted for and are actively looking for help.

I don't think we need to go into detail on this category. What is important to note is that if the prospect does have active needs (the tip-off that they might is that they called you), list this option first in your options section. You may also need to come prepared with a separate, specific solution, or at the very least, a detailed presentation on your company and the solution. A buyer who has active needs will want to address this area first, assessing whether you are the best choice.

Risk Mitigation Options

Risk Mitigation Options are the third type of option that may be included in a General Recommendations document. Risk Mitigation Options are meant to be appealing to buyers who now have active needs because of the progression through the General Recommendations, but who are not yet ready to accept the risk or burden of a full rollout of a solution. In other words, they want to hedge their bets.

The logic behind Risk Mitigation Options is as follows: "We think that you should buy Solution A in order to achieve your desired outcome and satisfy your active need. But we recognize that committing to a full rollout of Solution A might be too risky right now. Therefore, we've designed another option to help you determine if Solution A really can deliver what we say it can deliver."

One obvious example of a Risk Mitigation Option is a trial. Such an option would be to allow the customer to have access to the product or service for a defined period of time in order to get a sense of how it works, how difficult is it to learn and implement, and how effective it can be for the buyer organization.

Below is a short list of options one might suggest to a customer or prospect to gain the type of important buyer commitment that significantly advances the selling cycle.

- **Brainstorming sessions (demand creation option):** Brainstorming among key people of both organizations on a critical Blue Ocean client objective
- **Technology road map (demand creation option):** Showing clients what is technologically possible and how they might apply new processes to their business to change the game
- **Business process analysis (demand creation and/or risk mitigation option):** Assessing how the client currently gets important work done and generating a subsequent report detailing how this might be improved
- **Change studies (demand creation option):** Determining if change makes sense and conducting a study to help answer this question

- **Strategy symposium (demand creation option):** A gathering meant to help the client ideate on a mission critical area of their business
- **Internal or external survey (risk mitigation option or demand creation option):** Conducting an objective, third-party survey that helps the client better read the pulse of associates, stakeholders, and customers
- **Business summit (demand creation option):** Holding a high-level conference for executives to expand their horizons of best practices through exposure to speakers, workshops, subject matter experts, and peers
- **Test pilots (risk mitigation option):** Partnering with the client to test a new offering, experience a new technology, or validate a new offering category
- **Best solution study (service demand option):** Often, shopping-stage buyers do not understand how to make the best decision. In these cases, they often hire experts to study the situation and deliver a recommendation
- **Proposals (service demand option)**
- **Site visits (service demand option)**

EXERCISE

See if you can create three different suggestions—one for each type of option—that you might offer to an executive in the General Recommendations step.

PROGRESS!

Now, how do you end this important second meeting? This has been a very impressive display from the buyer perspective.

You've captured their situation remarkably well and have presented some very well-thought-out options. In other words, you've already added value. What now?

Very simply, no closing! What you must do instead is encourage the group to talk things through before they make a decision. In other words, please do not implode your entire effort by attempting to close on one or all of the options. Slow down the process by encouraging the key decision base to discuss your suggestions to determine the best course of action. Then simply agree on a date in the (near) future when they can give you commitment or direction.

And, that's it—you're done! From their perspective, if you were a salesperson at the beginning of this meeting, that person no longer exists. You are now a client advisor. You have set the table for a game change.

CHAPTER ELEVEN
DIFFERENCE MAKER

To create different kinds of customer value, our salespeople need to think differently.
I think this starts with being insatiably curious. You also need to be genuine.
Salespeople should forget using any "clever" sales techniques that might come
across as disingenuous or manipulative to the customer. This might net them a sale
in the short term, but it will hurt everyone in the long run. In other words, just be
you, and focus on helping the customer. This is not a sales mind—it's a mind-set.

—Tom Swidarsky, chief executive officer, Diebold

CONGRATULATIONS! YOU MAY NOT REALIZE IT, but if you just
follow the simple steps described in this book, everything will
change. Step-by-step, inch by inch, it really is a cinch. Just pour
yourself into learning the mind-set, strategies, and skills taught
in these pages and you will be on your way.

Discovery and General Recommendations may seem simple
on the surface, but executing these two steps properly requires
some practice and diligence. The General Recommendations process ultimately allows you and your client prospects to agree on
logical options that push the relationship forward. The options
you present are always carefully considered. And, depending on
which option(s) the buyer chooses, a new selling cycle is often
born, one that has a distinct life of its own.

For instance, let's assume that the group of people you've met
with agree to your company doing a functional analysis—an

assessment of their manufacturing processes to see if change might make sense. They have agreed to pay for this. At this point, your consulting team would engage, going through their analytic protocol (of course, if you're a small company, you may be the one doing the analysis). This would eventually lead to a deliverable, usually a report detailing the realities of the client situation—what's working, what's not, lost dollars, ROI, etc. Perhaps a statement of work might be included as part of this report—a proposal that would detail how the relationship might move forward around implementation of your new technology.

The point is that each option you present in a General Recommendations document will lead you and the client down a distinctive path. At this point, though, you're playing an entirely different game. No longer is your strategy emergent—that is, largely improvised due to unknown circumstances (like a first-call Discovery strategy). Rather, by the time options are presented and accepted, strategy has turned deliberate. Deliberate strategy implies that much is now known—situations, facts, and circumstances—allowing for the creation of strategy whose path and outcome are much more predictable. Of course, this is now possible due to the information you discovered during FOCAS and General Recommendations. Although all salespeople prefer to deal in deliberate strategic situations—shopping-stage situations where the buyer has an active need for your solution—it is the ability to navigate the unknown—the sandbox of emergent strategy—that truly separates businesspeople who sell from their average counterparts.

Put another way, discovery and General Recommendations are truly catalytic type sales calls. They enable you to gain the most difficult advantage of all—buyer momentum. Without momentum, an opportunity never gets off the ground. It's pretty

easy to work on an identified problem. It's infinitely more difficult to work in environments where there is no identified opportunity or problem—and emerge with actual momentum that can
eventually turn "potential" into "actual."

Equally important, the process you've just learned is truly
consultative. Almost all salespeople think of themselves as consultative, but few are. From the perspective of customer executives, most "consultants" are thinly veiled salespeople—wolves
in sheep's clothing. When you apply the process you have learned
in these pages, you will separate yourself by leaps and bounds
from all those eager to make a short-term sale. Remember, customer executives need help—just a different kind of help. They
are begging and pleading for people like yourself who can help
them differentiate and become more productive. Embracing this
mind-set, and following this process, is not only how you gain a
seat at their table, it is also how you become irreplaceable.

> **EXERCISE**
>
> Although most salespeople might describe themselves as "con-
> sultative," what do you feel truly makes a salesperson consulta-
> tive? To stimulate your thinking, how do you think your customers
> would answer the question "What makes a salesperson who calls
> on you truly consultative in today's new world?"

Although some consider "the seat" metaphorical, I consider
it very, very real. When executives who lead companies say that
you really made a big impact, they are indirectly telling you that
you have gained a seat at their table. This table is reserved for
those special *businesspeople* who have made a profound impact
on both the executives' personnel and their enterprises.

Helping your clients in new and different ways is really your ultimate award, and there could be no better or higher reward. Remember, you can make a huge difference in their lives.

- Customers want help—just a different kind of help.
- Customers want their businesses to become more productive and differentiated.
- Customers want to conceive of different products, capture different markets, and create new forms of value for *their* customers.

But until you become a *businessperson* who sells, the client will never see you as being different. You will be viewed as a salesperson, a strategic account manager, a CSR, a sales engineer, a technical specialist, or even a sales consultant—all traditional roles played by traditional people who deliver traditional results. You will be uninteresting, underwhelming, and unnecessary. *An expense.* Nothing could be worse.

On the flip side, when you help a client achieve a differentiated position, you will be viewed as something entirely different—a change agent, a strategic consultant, or a client advisor. You will be interesting, important, and impactful. Not only will you be sought out, you will also stand out. *An investment.* Nothing could be better. You will be seen as a difference maker, and the difference is profound.

The future for us is in our own place, if we can just learn to see it differently—and are strong in will to change it.

—Homer's *The Odyssey* (Note: Odysseus eventually returned home.)

Today, the only thing your customer cares about is value.

Want More Game-Changing Strategy and Insight?

Subscribe to Marc Miller's blog and tap into the very latest about today's most successful organizations and how they're engaging the executive level to drive decisions and win more business.

www.MarcMillerBlogs.com

More about the Sogistics Smartpen©

Chapter 6 has been generating lots of calls from sales executives looking to apply the Sogistics Smartpen© technology to evaluate sales calls, provide more timely and focused feedback, and ultimately drive better outcomes in the field. We've assembled a website where you can walk through a number of ways to put this technology to best use for your team.

www.SogisticsSmartpen.com